The
DEAD BRIDE

What Will Christ Find When He Returns for His Bride?

Mark Heikkila

Edited by Ellen Brock

WestBow
PRESS
A DIVISION OF THOMAS NELSON

WestBow Press books may be ordered through booksellers or by contacting:

WestBow Press
A Division of Thomas Nelson
1663 Liberty Drive
Bloomington, IN 47403
www.westbowpress.com
1-(866) 928-1240

ISBN: 978-1-4497-6157-8 (sc)
ISBN: 978-1-4497-6158-5 (hc)
ISBN: 978-1-4497-6156-1 (e)

Library of Congress Control Number: 2012914095

Printed in the United States of America

WestBow Press rev. date: 09/06/2012

TABLE OF CONTENTS

THANK YOU

Jesus. You lived a perfect life. You gave your very best. You gave your all. You carried out the Father's plan. You did nothing wrong, you served, you taught, you healed and yet, they killed you. It is scandalous, unfair, and unbelievable. Yet the more I think about it and if I were honest, if I were alive back then, I probably would have done it too. So I need to shift my posture to my knees and say thank you. Thank you for forgiving me, for taking my place in dying a horrific and brutal murderous death. You paid a debt you did not owe because I owed a debt I could not pay. I am forever grateful. Thank you for adopting me, for showing me the way, and for sending the Holy Spirit to guide, counsel, and comfort me in some pretty rough times. Where would I be without you? In a word . . . *lost!*

My wife Teresa. You are a gift from heaven and a dream come true. I can't believe I wake up next to you every morning. Thank you for loving me and teaching me about the nurturing side of God. I cannot believe the courage you display sometimes in serving God. The risks you take are both amazing and impressive. Thank you for your patience, your love, your companionship, and support. You really are my BFF . . . forever and always, triangle, square. Remember, "The best is yet to come."

Josh and Caleb ... the two good spies. God could not have blessed a man with better sons. You are both valiant warriors and I am honored to call you my sons. I cannot imagine life without either of you. You both hold so much promise and I love watching you become the men of God He has called you to be. No matter what the majority says, you keep your eyes on God and always worship Him in Spirit and in truth.

The staff of Jubilee Fellowship Church. You have no idea of where I was when I came to your doors nor do you know how you have altered our family tree. Thank you for being faithful to God's word and for sharing tough truths in a gracious manner. My life and my family will never be the same.

Jackie and Stan Jacobsen. Jackie, thank you for showing us how to walk led by the Spirit as a way of life. Thank you for your raging passion to teach the word of God in its purity, simplicity, and in humility. I am still a "Dead man walking!" Stan, you are an amazing servant. You teach more in your silent humility than I have taught in my lifetime. There is no doubt; God has put you two together to change the world.

Ellen Brock, my editor at Key Top Services. Thanks for making this work presentable. I am confident God brought you into my life at just the right time for such a time as this. Thanks for your work, for making me look like a bona fide author, and most of all your patience! If this one flies, are you up for a sequel?

THE WAIT

The desert was so hot during the day, and the nights weren't much better. The sand and wind were sometimes unbearable. There was never a moment to relax with the enemy waiting out there somewhere, murder as their goal. The days seemed so long, and the nights even longer. There were times when all he wanted to do was go home. He wanted to give up, to give in. But that was not in his nature; that was not what he signed up for. He wasn't a quitter. His father had taught him better than to be dishonorable. It was cowardly. He'd never quit on anything before, and he was not about to start now. He had to see this mission through to the end, otherwise he would let his squad down, and he would let her down too.

Her. In reality it was her that kept him grinding it out day after long, hot day, night after long, cold, lonely night. He could see her. He dreamed about her many times. Her skin was perfect; she could've been on the front of a fashion magazine. Her smile made something turn inside him. No matter how bad it got, a simple thought, a vision of her smile . . . wow. It brought a smile to his face and a bounce to his step. Her eyes were like nothing he had ever experienced growing up in a small town. She was so beautiful. She was perfect. Of course there were other pretty girls but none quite like her. The moment he laid eyes on her he longed for nothing more in the entire world than to be with her forever. He had done so much to meet her, to get to know her, to win her hand and her heart in marriage.

But others had a plan that altered their course. Deep inside, he knew he was in this god-forsaken desert for the right reasons. He was here to serve, to rescue, and somehow, deep down inside, he was actually here *for* her. Through every mission he kept thinking, *I have to get through this for her. I need to see her again.* There were close calls for sure. Incoming fire had once taken out half his men. Had it not been for aerial reinforcements raining fire from above, he might not have survived. It was the closest he had ever been to death's doors, and he didn't want to visit again.

He kept her photo nearby; it was a treasure, one of few he was able to keep in the desert. He cherished her letters and the rare times they Skyped. They were brief, but precious beyond even the water he drank. How could he be so lucky as to have her? She was so much more than a dream come true; she was a gift from heaven. She was his best friend ever, his one and only soul mate. It was almost as if life without her was not even life, it was simply existence.

As hard as it was to believe he had her, he could not figure out why he would leave her. She mentioned many times in her letters that she did not understand why he had to go. They had just begun to really get to know each other, and their love seemed so perfect. But he felt so obligated by duty that his very nature compelled him to go and fight this war. Injustice called to his heart. When someone else throws the first punch, well, you just can't do that without consequences. His dad taught him to never strike first, but when someone else strikes, well, it's on. It was that protective nature, that sense of right and wrong, a true sense of justice, which led him to fight back. Nobody would mess with his country, his rights, the rights of his family, fellow men, and yes, nobody would take away her rights either. To whom much was given, much was required. He owed it to his fellow men to engage the enemy and defeat them. That is the heart of the warrior, the essence of masculinity, humility, and service in action. The human spirit deserves freedom, and he would protect it at all costs, including his own life. Freedom would vanish if he sat back and allowed evil to prevail. Yet all of that seemed so foolish, false bravado at times, and he longed so badly to see her, to touch her face, kiss her lips. He'd give anything just to hold her in his arms for a moment.

The tour of duty seemed like an eternity. But alas, one day it was finally over. His time had come, and he was on his way home. The plane ride seemed as long as his term. He could not wait to look into her beautiful brown eyes again and to hold her close. It was as if he could smell her sweet fragrance right there in the plane. He looked at his watch and wished teleportation were reality. This trip could not go fast enough. What would he do when he first saw her? He could practically taste her kiss, sweet as the first time their lips met. He was nervous during that first kiss, like a scared junior high boy asking the prettiest girl in class to the dance. He smiled, they'd come a long way since that day. He checked his watch again.

"Hang on there, big guy. She'll be there when you get there," one of his comrades said, snickering "Checking the old wristwatch doesn't make it come any faster."

He smiled. His fellow warrior was right; you can't make water boil sooner by watching it.

The years apart were brutal, but she was worth it. Other guys in his team ridiculed him for his faithfulness. "Ahh, she will never know." "Everyone slips at some time." "It's what we do; it's who we are. Nobody could possibly be with one person their whole life." "Look what we go through out here, she'll understand." "Stop being so 'old fashioned'." These were the lines that made him cringe.

What drove him? Was it his honor? A vow he made? A promise to be kept? Was it just a vow or a promise for the sake of keeping a vow? Was it his love for her? He could not imagine the conversation if he had to tell her that he had not remained faithful while away. It wasn't hard for him. He loved her so much, and she was so worthy of that love, perfect and unblemished. The guys laughed when they told him, "She's probably having her fun too." He thought to himself, *It doesn't matter; I love her. Our love is strong. Our love is real. It will stand against anything, even the desert and the time apart. Even if she was unfaithful, we would figure it out. I can't live without her.* None of that mattered anymore. It was all about to be history, just a distant memory. Soon enough he would be in her arms, and he'd make up for all the lost time. They'd enjoy each other's embrace, and life would be back to perfect.

The plane touched down, and the wheels let off the familiar squeal as if to say "Welcome home, all is well!" At first he didn't know what meant more, being back on his home soil or seeing her; definitely seeing her.

Though he was only carrying a few small packs, he couldn't get his gear and get off of the plane fast enough. His heart raced. As he stepped off the plane, his eyes scanned the crowd. He'd recognize that amazing smile in a heartbeat. His biggest fear was running over a few soldiers or one of their family members in the hot pursuit to see her.

But something was wrong. He scanned the crowd once, then twice. She wasn't there. Maybe she cut or dyed her hair. Was she hiding behind someone to surprise him? She had that playful sort of teasing spirit that drove him nuts. Certainly anything she would have done wouldn't fool him. He knew her too well. He knew those eyes and that smile. His heart raced as he thought in disbelief, *She isn't here.* How could she be late for his arrival? There had to be a mistake. He looked again and again, but the only thing he saw were all of his fellow countrymen embracing their families, tears of relief and joy flowing, because they were so happy to see each other again. This is what he had waited for. One turned and left, and then another. Off into the distance they went, looking complete. Their dreams and plans that were put on hold were about to finally come to life. The long pause was over. Life could continue again as it was intended.

Something was wrong. Maybe she was just late. Perhaps they hadn't communicated clearly what time he would arrive. Did she think it was a different time or another day? This was the only place soldiers came home to. Certainly she knew that. Something *had* to be wrong. With great concern he rushed out and hailed a taxi, gave the driver his home address, put his belongings in the car, and headed off toward their home.

Maybe she is sick? Certainly she knew today is the day? They had talked and prepared for this day for so long, playing the scenario over and over again. *Something must be wrong.*

His mind raced. The thoughts darted all over; the stream of consciousness took him all through the desert, back to the barracks, and back to the desert, again and again. Now that he thought about it, her letters had begun to fade off. First he'd get a letter a day, sometimes two, and often tear-stained. But she mentioned that she found herself struggling to make time to write as often, and sometimes she ran out of things to say. He could understand then why the letters were less and eventually dwindled to one a week and sometimes even fewer. His heart sank. Perhaps they had drifted apart after all? Maybe she had found another man, and he was the fool on the outside? *Oh no, it can't be. No way.* It became hard to breathe.

He had forgotten how bad traffic could be in this town. It was taking so long to get home. He noticed the familiar sights, the old buildings that had been renovated, painted, and patched. New buildings appeared in places where there were none before. Things change, yet they stay the same. None of it mattered as his head fogged with confusion. Where was she? Why didn't she meet him at the airport? Deep inside he still longed so badly to see her. It had been so long since he was home, so long since he'd seen her beautiful face. There had to be a logical explanation.

The last time they'd Skyped, she didn't look well, didn't look herself. She seemed a bit tired, distracted, and almost irritable. When he asked her what was wrong she brushed it off and simply said she wasn't feeling well. He should have noticed. He should have pushed harder to find out if something was really wrong. Had she gotten sick? Did she have something terminal and didn't want to tell him? Was she in the hospital? Of course, that was why she didn't come to the airbase to see him. How sick was she? Why didn't she tell him? She could have left a message. Was she okay? He reached forward to tell the taxi driver to go to the hospital but thought better of the idea.

At last they turned the corner off the interstate and were heading into his neighborhood. The short fifteen-mile drive from the airbase to his home seemed longer than the nineteen-hour flight over the desert and the pond. Finally they pulled onto his street. He saw their house. That cute, little white house with the picket fence; their little kingdom. He couldn't believe his eyes; she had decorated it for his return! But as they got closer it became clear that the decorations were tattered, rain-soaked, worn and falling down. It looked like she had put them up years ago.

He pulled up to the front sidewalk. The signs and streamers were wet, smudged, and falling apart. She had been expecting him, but that was clearly a long time ago. The rain and weather had nearly ruined the welcome sign she'd made for him. She wasn't there to greet him at the door. This wasn't what he had planned. This wasn't what he had envisioned for years. His head spun.

The neighborhood was surreal as the taxi pulled away and left him alone in front of his home with his belongings. He stood in stunned silence as if standing there would solicit her to the front door. How had this momentous occasion gone so wrong in such a short time? He had gone halfway around the world to see his wife, and she wasn't there.

He approached the door and found it dislodged. Had someone broken in? The door jamb appeared untouched; there was no sign of forced entry. Had she been kidnapped? Were the intruders still there? He pushed the door the rest of the way open and stood in silence, waiting to hear anything. His mind was a ball of confusion and fear, but he managed to reach down deep inside and ask in a quiet voice, "Anybody home?" No answer. Had she slipped out? Maybe they had crossed paths on the way from the air base?

The house was a mess. It was unlike her to leave the place in such a disorganized and jumbled condition. She was a neat freak, almost to a fault. But dirty laundry laid on the floor, old newspapers mingled with magazines and junk mail on the table, dishes were scattered.

There was not a sound outside of his own labored breathing. As he made his way to the living room, he announced, "Honey, I am home!" As he rounded the corner he couldn't believe his eyes. He gasped. There she was . . . face down, asleep on the couch! *Are you kidding me?* He thought, *I am scared half to death and thinking a million cluttered thoughts, and she sleeps on the couch. Oh boy, she's never going to live this one down, not in a million years.* It gave him an arsenal of ammunition for future mistakes.

He exclaimed in joy, "Wow, all this time I have been anticipating this day and here you are asleep on the couch. A guy comes halfway around the world to see his bride and she . . ." She wasn't stirring. She wasn't moving at all.

He rushed to the couch and looked more closely. She wasn't breathing. Her eyes looked sunken, her face pale and lifeless. He touched her lips, and they were cold, blue, and lifeless. His heart started beating out of his chest. What had happened? The thoughts raced in his mind, adrenaline coursing through his veins. *I am a highly trained operative and have seen many wounded soldiers in the line of battle, but what do I do? Is she dead? Do I call 911? How long has she been this way?* He shook her gently; he called her name softly. No response. She just laid there unresponsive. He shouted her name louder and louder, escalating into screams of fear and panic.

In desperation, he began CPR, his lips pressed against her cold lips. He wept. He cried out, "No! Why? What happened? Who did this?"

In panic, he called 911 and pleaded with the dispatcher on the other end to get someone there immediately. He dropped the phone to the floor and fell on her cold, lifeless body, weeping gut-wrenching sobs of unbelievable pain. His bride, his love . . . how could this have happened? It couldn't be. This was not what he had planned for so long. This dream had become a nightmare.

Who did this? He had to get revenge. He had to stop at nothing to avenge her death. He had to seek them out. They must pay, and they have to die. He looked at her, and she looked a mess. It wasn't how it was supposed to be. As the sirens approached in the distance he wept bitterly over his bride, his love, his friend . . . his loss. He wept bitterly and painfully. He wept so hard he was barely able to breathe. He doubled over and fell into a fetal position on the floor. He had never wept in such agony before.

A DREAM GONE SOUTH

Did you feel his pain? You did, didn't you? A made for movie moment that was supposed to be filled with tears of joy suddenly became a horror show. Our man expected his bride, his lover, the woman of his dreams to greet him upon his arrival. Instead death's cold breath exhaled upon his dreams.

The first chapter poses a enormous question facing the world today. What will Jesus Christ find when He returns to earth? What condition will His bride be in upon His return? Will He too be greeted with the cold reality that His bride has died?

As you read this book you might feel offended. You might ask yourself, "Who is this guy to criticize the church of God?" I want to begin by saying that I myself am surprised that I've written this book. I ask the same question as you, "Who am I to write a book about the bride of Christ?" Those who are close to me are more surprised than both of us. "Mark writing a book?" They know that more than once I had a yearly goal to *read* a book.

Maybe you are a pastor and you take a lot of pride in your ministry. You work long hours to tend to the sheep. You labor over God's word week after week, and you feel the pain of a "cold bride". Maybe you will feel attacked by this book. Maybe you will even fire off a shot at me, "Yeah, you think you could do better? Bring it!"

Perhaps you are an elder in the church or a Sunday school teacher. Perhaps you work in children's church or the youth ministry, and you hold a full-time job too. Maybe you do all of the above. As you read you may feel the skin on your face flushing with anger. "How dare you talk about the bride like that?"

I want to begin by asking you to put this book down and do something. I will ask you to do this multiple times as you read. It might be best to read alone. I want you to pray before moving ahead. I want you to speak (maybe for the first time in this manner) with the Holy Spirit of God, and ask Him to speak to you as you read this book. Ask Him to decode and decipher these words, and ask Him to shine His light on the truth. Ask Him to speak truth into your life regarding the bride of Christ, His blood bought bride.

You see, I didn't want to write this book. It's my first book, and, truth be told, I have been avoiding it for a while. I have been on a personal journey of transformation and brokenness, and after fifteen years "in the wilderness" I emerge to comfort the afflicted and to afflict the comforted. I have struggled with this topic, and truthfully some have told me I dare not go here. I run the risk of saying some things that will get me in trouble.

However, I have always felt that as a minister of the gospel, I have not been called to win a popularity contest; I have been called to present the truth as I best believe God is speaking to me. In the past, I might not have been gracious at all. I believe that my last fifteen years in the wilderness have been to temper my passions and to bring me to a place of humility. At times it felt like my life was a train wreck, and the last thing I thought I would be doing is writing a book of this type and about this topic.

Let me take you back in time a bit. As a young minister, I was full of zeal and passion. I wanted so badly for the bride of Christ to rise up and impact the world around her. I heaped loads of legalism, guilt, and duty, with a healthy dose of discipline, upon those in my care. When people wouldn't toe the line or fulfill my expectations, I would get frustrated and even angry. I couldn't figure out why they couldn't be like me and "get it". I am embarrassed to look back at those whom the Lord entrusted to me and how I walked for years embracing my own ideas and man-made philosophies instead of bringing the power the apostle Paul spoke of in 1 Corinthians 2:1-5.

> *"And when I came to you, brethren, I did not come with superiority of speech or of wisdom, proclaiming to you the testimony of God. For I determined to know nothing among you except Jesus Christ, and Him crucified. I was with you in weakness and in fear and in much trembling, and my message and my preaching were not in persuasive words of wisdom, but in demonstration of the Spirit and of power, so that your faith would not rest on the wisdom of men, but on the power of God."*

I did not come in the Spirit or in the Spirit's power. Instead I came in my own flesh, full of my ideas and what I was convinced all people needed to hear. I fear that my epitaph could have read, "He was a man of God, however . . ." That "However" part is something a true man of God would never want because it would probably be sung in a Sinatra like tune, "He did it his way and in his own strength."

So I come to you today and run the risk of offending you. I admit from the beginning, I do not feel qualified nor do I feel I have all of the answers. I hope you can remember that as you read this book. This book is just a primer to get you thinking. I want this to be the type of work that says, "Come, let us reason together".

I need to say very boldly from the beginning of this adventure that I neither am trying to attack anyone nor am I trying to criticize legitimate works of God or any of His servants. I applaud you as you serve Him faithfully, the best you know how with tired hands and a heavy heart. I know many who read this book will do so with weary eyes from serving Him with every fiber of their being. I am not calling into question anyone or any ministry specifically. Again, I ask before you read on, be certain that you are in a position to hear from the Holy Spirit and hear only what He has to say to you (Revelation 2:29, 3:6,13 & 22).

I cannot say this clearly or often enough. I am not taking a shot at anyone in what I am writing. I know myself to be anything but perfect. The last thing I want to do is assault Christ's bride. I am not *that* guy. I am trying to address this situation in humility, realizing that Christ loves His bride and is jealous about her, and I warn anyone who would try to take a shot at His lady. Jesus knows His bride isn't perfect. He knows she has her issues, but He loves her with passion and purity. Christ, through the Father's plan, didn't pay for her with the minimum left-over change He had lying around on the nightstand. He gave His all. He emptied out the coffers to buy her. He spared nothing. He gave it all, and He held nothing back for her ransom. So I tread lightly and respectfully, knowing that He loves her despite her flaws.

For about fifteen years I was out of full-time Christian service. I originally began in the ministry as a youth pastor, then moved on for a short time to public speaking, then later found myself without resources in a full-time job in the construction industry. I was warned by a loving mentor about getting too involved in business and losing sight of the ministry as I made more money. During those fifteen years a deep battle raged within me as I felt I was not being true to my calling as a minister. Yet every time I tried to get back into the ministry full-time, the doors were closed. I cried out to God many times asking Him why I was wasting my time in the "wilderness" of the marketplace. About the same time I began writing this book, the Holy Spirit revealed what He was doing in my life. If I am to be honest with you, those fifteen years were a "time out" for me. I have a confession to make: I used to beat up the bride of Christ.

I am both sickened and ashamed of myself when I think back on the things I used to heap upon the children of God. I look back at years of legalistic teachings that came from my lips and burdens I imposed upon brothers and sisters, and I nearly weep. Please understand, I wasn't asked to leave the full-time ministry. I was applauded for what I said and did. I was reminded often how much potential I had as a speaker and what a great and faithful pastor I was. Even years later when I spoke of this with young people I ministered to, that are now in the ministry, they say they didn't see anything missing. They thought things were fine. I pray that the grace of God protected them from me. I used to abuse the bride of Christ and strangely enough, she applauded it.

What the Spirit revealed to me was that He loves His bride and loved me and would not allow the abusive relationship to continue. He put me in "time out" to illustrate my arrogance, my legalistic and abusive ways, and ultimately to bring me to a point of humility and love for her. He loves His bride and would not allow me to make a fool of her or myself nor would He, in His love, allow me to continue to harm her.

So, I am not approaching this as another beating for the bride. I do not seek to condemn or come across as condescending. I have come to see the bride of Christ from a very different perspective, and I long to see her live her destiny and be the beautiful, powerful, unspotted bride she is called to be. My writing is a humble attempt to be obedient to what I think I have been called to do: address a serious problem leading to a helpful outcome. I pray this book is but a small piece that is used to help get us where we need to be, awake and vibrant.

The purpose of this book is to point out a scenario that I believe God has called me to address. Plain and simple, I believe that the bride of Christ is either dead or mortally wounded. I will attempt in the pages that follow to explain why I believe this, to describe how we got to this point, and to shed some light on the more important issue of where we go from here.

We have a real problem. We are blind, destitute, and naked, yet we think we are in need of nothing (Revelation 3:17-18). Somehow, some way we have become wounded or have died. The Groom, Christ, is coming. Many believe it is soon, and when He returns, what will He find (Matthew 25:5 & 6)? We have somehow lost touch with a dead and dying world to the point that we are by and large irrelevant. We have lost sight of the fact that hell is hot, and it is still there waiting to consume those who enter eternity without Christ at the center of their heart and passions. We find ourselves so wrapped up in our day to day lives, with minimal attendance and less involvement at church, and perhaps we believe there is nothing of substance there when we get arrive at church. Somehow the world has sucked the life out of us, and we have slipped into a coma, and we don't even know it. It is like we are stuck in an early scene of the movie "The Matrix", and we are hooked to tubes and wires, not really alive, but we don't even know it. We have lost sight of the fact that Christ is coming! We are His bride. We have died, and we don't even know it!

I will say it one more time. The one who writes this book is not pointing a finger. The dude rowing the boat beside you . . . that's me! I do not stand in judgment of you, your church, or those around you. If you come to a point in this book where you get offended, stop and ask the Holy Spirit a simple question, "Why? Why does it bug me? Why am I offended? What is getting at me?"

What is the reason for the book? The groom is coming . . .

A DEAD BRIDE

In the New Testament Jesus refers to His body as His bride. He seems to take special delight in the fact that we are His bride. Stop and think about that for a minute. *You* are the bride of Christ. Seriously, stop and think deeply about this concept. The rest of the book is worthless if you don't understand this. You are the bride of Jesus Christ.

I think that is a big part of the problem with the church today and why I feel that the Lord called me to put it in print. The bride of Christ doesn't see herself that way. Maybe you are a lady reading this book, and you struggle to see yourself as the bride of Christ, because you are in a broken relationship (maybe multiple times over), and your wedding day was the only good thing about your marriage. I am sorry that happened to you. However, please read on.

Maybe you are a man and think the whole bride thing doesn't fit you, because it's too girly. Well, I will do my best to help you see that it really does apply to you and that it's important for you to understand it.

Sometimes it is hard to see ourselves as the bride. To try to get us there, let's stop and do some reflecting. Think about that time when you really fell in love. I can remember the first day I met my wife Teresa. She was sitting there in a moment ordained by God, looking beautiful outside the cafeteria at our college in Virginia. I was chasing another girl and making the point that I could have any girl I wanted (remember that part about being young and needing humility? Is it starting to come into focus yet?). I turned to the one I was pursuing and pointed to Teresa and said, "Like her. I could ask her if she wanted to go out with me and she would." I turned to Teresa and asked, "Right?" At that moment, I believed there was a God in heaven because she said "Yes". I looked away for a second, then looked back and said in a surprised voice, "What did you say?"

Two weeks later I met her in the hallway between classes and, like any broke college guy, asked her out for pizza. Again, I was surprised that she agreed to go with me. That day was like a day in heaven. We talked so much and shared as if we were long lost friends. I remember that night saying to God, "I will do *anything*, yes, even be a missionary, just make her mine!"

I am not one for love at first sight, but that's what it felt like. I thought about her all the time. I wanted to be with her. I wrote her letters and longed to read the ones she'd written me. That was before email, social media, Skype, and all the forms of connection we have today. I can only imagine how much we would have contacted each other had we had those options. While we were apart I would get the mail everyday from the mailbox hoping for a letter from her. I would get defensive if anyone said anything about her that was wrong or even questionable. I told my buddies she was so amazing, "I'd drink her bath water!", though I am not sure what that would have accomplished. I was head over heels, sunk, sick, whipped, and everything else you could say about me.

Do you remember that time in your life? I want to tell you something right now. Maybe you have heard this before. Maybe this has settled in your heart or perhaps, like me, for the longest time you heard this, but you never really *heard* it: that's how Jesus loves you! That's right; The Almighty is madly in love with you. The King of Kings is waiting to come and be with you. The Lord of Lords has your name written on

His hand, and He cannot wait to be with you because of His amazing love for you. The nation of Israel once felt as if God had forgotten them because of the long road of discovery they were on. God doesn't forget us. No matter how bad we mess it up, no matter how far we have run, He doesn't give up on us. Check this out from Isaiah 49:15 & 16.

> *"Can a woman forget her nursing child and have no compassion on the son of her womb? Even these may forget, but I will not forget you. Behold, I have inscribed you on the palms of My hands; Your walls are continually before Me."*

You may have picked up this book struggling to believe that you are even loved by God, let alone believing you are His precious bride for goodness sake. The thought of you actually being the bride of His choice in your mind is completely out of the question. You have run too far, you have done too much, and you feel that you don't deserve His love. But the facts are the facts. He loves you! Don't give up on Him, because He hasn't and won't give up on you. What did you do to deserve it? Absolutely nothing! It is because of His goodness. It is because of His nature. It is His grace extended to you. That's just like God. Right now you might not be there, but somehow you must come to terms with this. Almighty God loves you, and He has prepared a place for you and will come to get you so you can be together in His presence for eternity. That's a long time and a great thought for our small minds to handle.

By the way, did you know the Groom is coming back for His bride? That's right, He is coming back to get you soon. This is great news! Or is it?

Let's look at this with a golf analogy. If you are putting and your putter face is open a mere one degree, unless you have my luck, you will probably sink the putt. However, if you move seventy-five yards off the green swinging your pitching wedge and you are off one degree, you probably won't even land on the green. If you're teeing off with your driver 450 yards from the green and you are off one degree, you might end up in the water, the woods, or on someone else's fairway!

So what's my point? The further you go through life, off even ever so slightly in your belief system, the further off you get from truth and God's plan for your life. Some of you have drifted over time, and the game isn't much fun right now. You are taking your hacks and swings, and it seems like all you're doing is digging holes and making a mess.

Strangely enough, in the life of the church, we really aren't aware nor do we live in the reality that we are off base and not living to our holy calling and destiny. I am proposing in this book that the bride of Christ is virtually ineffective and irrelevant to the world around her. The poor remain in poverty. The lost remain lost. Hell gobbles up souls by the millions, and we go about our lives as if this is somehow acceptable or even pleasing to the Groom. We look at the great commission and our calling as a body and feel almost as if there was a calculated loss God was willing to take from the foundation of the world. Read the following passage from Revelation 3:17-18.

> "Because you say, "I am rich, and have become wealthy, and have need of nothing," and you do not know that you are wretched and miserable and poor and blind and naked, I advise you to buy from Me gold refined by fire so that you may become rich, and white garments so that you may clothe yourself, and that the shame of your nakedness will not be revealed; and eye salve to anoint your eyes so that you may."

We've become so familiar with scriptures like these that we think to ourselves, "Yeah, those Laodiceans were sure messed up. How in the world could they get it so wrong?" We don't even stop to think that the passage is really about us, right here today. We have become so intoxicated with pride that we stumble and fumble around, and we don't even know it. We think we are doing okay, and we think to ourselves, "We really aren't all that bad when you think about it. I mean, it could be worse, right?"

As some of you read this, it will resonate with you. Something has been missing for years. There is a missing piece (or shall I say peace). Some of you know you are dead or mortally wounded, and you are tired of it. Some of you want the abundant life that Jesus spoke of. You know somehow it is supposed to define your life, and you feel as if you've been ripped off or duped but cannot prove it. You are tired of living week to week, weekend in church after weekend in church, and nothing changes, no real progress is made. You are tired of the way things are, and you know something isn't right, but you don't know what it is. You feel as if you are on a treadmill running miles and miles yet getting nowhere. You are expending a great deal of energy and sweating yourself into oblivion. You are like Neo in the Matrix. It is like a "splinter in your brain, driving you mad", but you cannot figure out what is missing. You want out, but you are not sure what you want out of. You hunger for life. You read where Jesus said in John 10:10 that "I have come that they might have life, and that they might have it more abundantly." And you think to yourself, I want the life, forget about the abundant part, I just want life.

Well friend, I feel your pain. I have been there too. Unfortunately I still, at times, find myself there. If this is how you feel, then please friend, read on. I think somewhere in these pages God in the form of His Holy Spirit wants to meet with you, and if you persevere and keep seeking, He will find you! You may have run a million miles, but He is only a step away, because He pursues you. Remember, He loves you. You are His bride.

Somehow, the bride of Christ has gone comatose. Somehow she no longer has the life He gave her. Somehow she has lost sight of the fact that He is coming back for her. For some unfounded and silly reason she mistakenly believes that His return is so far away. It's almost as if His return is a fairy tale. He longs to see her unstained from the world, unaffected by the stench of death, yet here we are addressing that as the very thing that holds her captive. Somehow long ago, she got off track. Ever so slightly, over the course of time, she began to die, and she never knew it. She has become the proverbial frog boiling in the kettle.

Before I go on I want to take a step back and make something very clear. I am in no way saying that God, in His great love for us, *needs* us. There is a fine line here that gets blurred and crossed. What I am saying is His love is so intense, so amazing, deep, and wide that it is misunderstood. At the same time, His love is hard to grasp by some yet warped and abused by others. In our feeble attempts to describe the amazing love of God we miss it on both sides of the issue. We weaken it, and we also overstep our boundaries when it comes to the nature of God. Both are disastrous. In case there is any doubt I want to make this very clear, God doesn't *need* us; He wants us. There is a huge difference.

I fear another misconception that is prevalent in the church's teachings is that God is somehow incomplete and needs us or our response to His love to fulfill Himself. Some would adopt, teach, believe, and practice a doctrine that our rejection of His love somehow leaves Him sobbing in heaven, wishing we would be His valentine and therefore make His day. God in and of Himself needs *nothing*. He alone is fully complete in and of Himself; he lacks and needs nothing. Otherwise He wouldn't be God. He created us for His glory and joy, not to fulfill a void in His life or character. If every single human on the face of the earth were an atheist and utterly rejected God, it would not make Him one ounce less God than He is. He does not need our acceptance, our service, or our hearts to somehow improve Himself or His status as God. Because of His grace, He simply loves us and wants a relationship with us. It is humbling and amazing to think of it: the Creator of all things past, present and future loves me and longs to be in a relationship with me. Stranger yet is to think that anyone would reject an offer like that.

With all of this in place, let's move on to see if we can uncover what happened to our bride. The pages that follow are a humble attempt to discover what happened. How did she die? Whom or what killed the dearly loved bride of Christ? Maybe more importantly, what can be done about it? Can she be resuscitated or is it too late? Has she gone too far?

ALWAYS CHECK THE
SPOUSE FIRST

Let's pull out our CSI kit and begin to investigate the facts to see if we can locate the criminal in this case.

We have on the couch one bride, the bride of Christ, and for all intents and purposes she is just laying there motionless.

When the police arrived at the scene of our deceased bride, the only other person there was a weeping husband dressed in military gear. As any good CSI agent would, they asked the spouse first.

But why in the world would God kill His own bride? This may be the most personal and humbling chapter for me to write. For years I honestly felt that God didn't *really* love me. In fact I believed in my heart that God "had it out for me." Despite the fact that I went to a bible college and served in ministry for nearly half of my life, it hasn't been until recently that I actually felt the love of God for the first time. I shudder to think that on more than one occasion in my life, out of pain and frustration, I actually called myself the "son of perdition". Things didn't go the way I wanted them to, or how I thought they should, so I became angry with God. At times I shook my fist at the heavens and yelled at God, wondering what He had against me. When I tried to do the "right thing" it seemed I always paid the price for it.

For a good portion of my life I adopted the phrase "no good deed goes unpunished". Another favorite saying of mine was "the beatings will continue until morale improves". I was convinced that God really had an axe to grind against me.

I sit back at times and wonder why I felt this way. Was it that I was so undeserving from past sins? I felt that even though Christ paid for my sins through the brutal murderous event at Calvary, for some reason it wasn't enough. I felt as if I hadn't done enough to deserve His love or I still owed some kind of debt and God was mad at me because I was behind on my payments or something. It was weird thinking, but it controlled me.

I think there are thousands of believers out there today that need this chapter perhaps more than any other in this book.

Perhaps the first time I came face to face with the idea that God didn't really care about me was back in college. During my entire high school career I played basketball, and every year I had to go to the local doctor to get a physical. From the seventh grade through my senior year, I knew I had a hernia but no doctor could find it. My metabolism was so active I looked like the poster child to end starvation yet I had this huge bulge in my abdomen.

When I hit the second semester of my freshman year of college, I tried to play basketball. The practices were grueling and much more difficult than anything I had come across in small town Ohio. The hernia was killing me. Many mornings I felt sick and just lay in bed, missing classes. I went to the campus doctor and as soon as he looked at it, he knew right away that was one bad hernia!

Well, if I am going to be truthful I won't blame it all on the hernia. I also had my fill of freshman laziness. I failed three of my five classes the second semester of my freshman year. While back home recovering from the massive hernia surgery (the doctor said he could put his fist through the tear in my abdominal wall) I received a letter from the college saying I was academically ineligible to receive financial aid because of my grades. I was so disillusioned. I felt that the physical problems were out of my control and that doctors should have made the proper diagnosis years before.

I then realized that I didn't have the money to return to college and therefore would not see my girlfriend/future wife again. I became very mad at God for allowing this to happen. Why didn't the doctors figure this out years ago? Why didn't God have the teachers pass me? They did say I would make it. Why didn't the school make it right where they were wrong? I reasoned to myself, *God, if you are so big, if you are so 'loving', why aren't you taking care of me?* In my anger, I spent the next year rebelling and running from God. I pointed out the errors in everyone in my church, including my pastors and parents. They were all hypocrites. During this time of my life seeds were planted that gave birth to some very broken and destructive theology and belief systems that would haunt me for years.

About ten years ago I had my own electrical contracting business. We founded the company on the basis of integrity and character. It was around the time the Enron scandals had broken the headlines, and we believed that there needed to be a contractor that people could trust to do good quality work at a fair price. We started with a used pickup truck and began building our business one customer at a time through word of mouth. We had no marketing budget, just a handshake, referrals, and references. We came across a mechanical contractor who lived in our neighborhood who was much like us, small and working out of their garage. His electrician was unreliable, and he wanted to give us a chance. We knew he and his family needed Christ and thought we could partner with them and grow our businesses together. I sent over pricing and said we'd love to work with him. He called back and said our rates were too high and that he couldn't sell his jobs with that much cost for electrical work. Since he was just getting started, and since we wanted to reach him for Christ, we lowered the rates and trusted God to make it work somehow. We worked for them for a couple of years, doing our very best and making very little money doing it. We even discounted the work further so they wouldn't lose money when they made a mistake on their bids. We ate dinner together as families, and our children played together and became friends.

One day while on a job, a customer changed where they wanted their air conditioner located. The mechanical contractor hadn't bid much in the job because the electrical circuit was very close to the panel. He asked us to "please go easy on me" with the cost of the change. I knew he was going to struggle to get more money from the client so I finished my work, submitted my bill with heavy discounts, and went on to another job. A few hours later I received a phone call from the customer. They were very upset and called my integrity into question. She said "... the job more than doubled and the mechanical contractor said it was all because of the electrician." My friend had lied to the customer and threw me under the bus. I saw him the next day on another job and challenged him over the facts the customer had presented to me. All he could do was shrug his shoulders and say, "Oh well."

A few weeks later our wives were driving the kids back from the local swimming pool when his wife asked mine, "How do you guys avoid paying all the taxes on six figures?" My wife was shocked, because we didn't make that kind of money, and asked, "Do you mean six figures of revenues or profits?" The mechanical contractor's wife responded, "Profit of course." We were blown away! We had been discounting our work, working so hard for these guys, and the whole thing was a scam. They were rolling in the dough at our expense. So I confronted the contractor friend again and asked for an explanation. Again, he shrugged his shoulders and said, "That's how money is made in business."

This is where I adopted the phrase "No good deed goes unpunished." So many times I would do what I felt was right, just, honest, and honorable before God only to be abused and taken advantage of. Again I reasoned that if God really loved me, and if I was a cherished son of His, if "His banner over me is love", then why is this garbage happening to me? I reasoned, *Hey God, if this is your love in action, don't do me any favors!*

I sometimes wonder if the idea that God is out to get me was planted spiritually by my grandmother years ago. Then again, maybe they were planted long before her time, and she inherited them. In her heart she has battled for years and struggled with God over one question. Books have been written and some of our brightest thinkers have mulled over my grandma's greatest heart cramp. How could a loving God allow such sin in this world to harm innocent children? Maybe you have heard someone else ask this question. Maybe you yourself have asked it, "If God were all powerful . . . ?" or "If God were all loving or all knowing . . . ?"

How could a good, loving, peaceful, kind God allow such atrocities? It is as if in the question there is really a statement of blame. In most cases it is not really a question, or it's at best a rhetorical one. I am not sure the people asking it are really seeking the answer. It is more about placing blame on God because things don't go the way we think they should. It is as if we think that God ought to supersede the choice of mankind and make all of us robots so we could get along with each other and be nice.

They want God to make everything right, to make us all be kind and get along but somehow do it without calling them into accountability. Do they know their request is really impossible? Do they not know that if God gives us free will that there are consequences to doing our own thing? It is ironic how we want to reject God and His laws yet we anticipate that a society without God will have no pain, wrong, or suffering. That just doesn't make sense.

In the heart of mankind lies a belief that we are not supposed to suffer. That life is supposed to be one big bowl of cherries surrounded by puppy dogs and flowers. Where does it say in the Bible anywhere that we will have that kind of life? Look throughout history and you will see the saints from the New Testament to saints all around the world today suffering greatly and even dying for their faith . . . including Christ! How did we get so off track in our thinking that we thought that God said we would never suffer? As a matter of fact, I would say that if you are in Christ you *will* most certainly suffer (2 Timothy 3:12), and if you are not suffering at all, you might want to do some introspection.

Why do we blame God for everything? After all didn't He, in His love, bless us with free will so that we could choose? From the Garden of Eden we chose to reject His love and choose our own ways instead. God offered to be the king of the nation of Israel, but they wanted a king made of flesh and blood, and now we have government and loathe every election and new law and tax. We rejected God's offer to rule us in His divine love and perfect plan and in its place choose our broken and defunct man-made plan. As a result we suffer the consequences and wonder why it all went wrong. We shoot God the proverbial bird, and we wonder why things are so bad.

Instead of sitting in the corner pouting about that "Big Mean God", let's think about another perspective. What if God uses the bad things that happen to good people to build character in them? God makes all things work together for our good (Romans 8:28). God has gone so far as to let us know very plainly, ". . . My thoughts are not your thoughts; My ways are not your ways (Isaiah 55:8)." So when things don't make sense, instead of looking at that scripture and saying, "Almighty God, help me understand, teach me, grow me, mold me, and develop character in me . . ." we get angry and become disillusioned, and some even turn their back on God and walk away in frustration.

Have you ever stopped to think that most of the time God's plan and ideas seem, well . . . crazy? Let me give you a few examples, and see if you might agree.

Moses and the children of Israel are fighting a battle. The battle is raging and going well for Israel as long as Moses holds his arms in the air. As soon as he lowers his arms, the battle changes, and the children of Israel begin to lose. Yeah right, I wish that worked all the time. We'd all just stand around with our arms in the air.

While on Moses, let's hit another one. They are being chased to the Red Sea by Pharaoh's army, about to be taken back into captivity or killed. With nowhere else to go, Moses raises his stick and this huge body of water opens up, and they walk across dry land! Again, have you ever had that one work for you?

How about this one? Joshua and the children of Israel are told to take the fortified city of Jericho. The battle plan is to march around the city tooting their horns and watching the walls implode. I know some worship leaders who believe they can pull that one off, but I am not so sure.

Naaman was riddled with leprosy and heard that the prophet of God could cleanse him. He goes to the prophet Elisha and is told to go take a bath in the muddy waters of the Jordan seven times (2 Kings 5). Have you ever washed off a disease in a mud puddle?

Friends, I don't know how else to say it, because God says it best, "My plans are not your plans and neither are My ways." I think it is very obvious that the aforementioned stories were not done by human plan and reason. They were miracles of God. God seems to put us in positions where He stacks the odds against us such that only He can do the miracle. How often do we rob ourselves of miracles because we lose sight of the fact that He is God and that He does love us? We are His bride, and He wants to do something special in our lives if we will seek Him and pursue Him with more than a casual approach.

I personally know of three instances where people in the church found themselves sucker punched by the sin of adultery. In each of these three instances it was the woman who was unfaithful and deeply wounded their man. In each instance the man wanted to, and had the right by God, to leave the marriage. Yet in all three, these men battled through the pain, even ignored counsel to leave their wives, and trusted God. In all three relationships these couples are not only still married, they are deeply in love, serving God and enjoying a deeper relationship with their spouse and their Savior than they ever thought possible. The easy thing to do, the thing the world would have had them do, would be to walk, start over, and try another spouse. But in these cases, these people trusted God, and He saved their family trees. How many times do we stop miracles from happening? How many times do we walk out on God when He is about to do a life-changing miracle? Not only that, but when we walk out on God, we turn around and blame Him! We get impatient, because God doesn't work as fast as we think He ought to.

I can think of many times in my own life (reflected in the stories I shared earlier in this chapter) when I was feeling angry with God. I rode out the storm and found later that it was there to build my character and to make me more like Christ. All I wanted was the easy life, no pain, no suffering, because if God really loved me I wouldn't suffer, right? How often do we operate out of our flesh and short circuit the work of God *to our own demise*? My pastor has said multiple times that disillusion is the mother of a lot of bad theology. We have low times and instead of looking to God and asking for His heart, we lean on our own understanding and become bitter.

I carried the belief that God was out to get me for a long time. I would have a bad day and I'd say things like, "See, no good deed goes unpunished" or "I told you! I know God is love, but He's ticked at me today." How silly I feel as I look back on those types of statements. I believed this lie for so long until I heard my pastor say, "If God was out to get you, don't you think He would have got you by now?" I almost chuckle now when I think about how I believed that lie. You see, Satan was whispering the lies to me, telling me that God didn't love me and that He was out to get me. All I was doing was empowering the lies, and the liar, by coming into agreement with him. I was imprisoning myself by believing them.

Do you know the best lies are mostly true? Do you know that the best thing to counteract a lie is to expose it to truth? Let me pull you back to some truth.

Look, there are no two ways about it, God loves you! He is not against you. He has great plans for you, plans to prosper you, to build His kingdom in and through you. You are a child of the Most High; you are royalty, not a beggar. You are a child of the King, and let me tell you, that's not hype! That's not some health, wealth, and prosperity gospel. That is just truth and fact and fact and truth. Don't weaken the truth by slapping a denominational name tag upon it. It is God's truth to you, His gift to His child. Why would you want anything else?

Maybe you are reading this book right now and you feel the sting of betrayal by a parent, a friend, or perhaps a spouse. Maybe a child has run away, maybe a spouse has left you. Don't blame God, don't push Him away. *Seek Him!* That's right, draw near to Him.

I have some martial arts experience. Many of the martial arts forms will train you to do the opposite of what your opponent thinks you will do. For instance, when someone walks up and grabs you by the collar like they are going to hit you, what is your natural tendency? To pull away in self defense, right? A good instructor will show you how to use your opponent's force against him. In other words, don't step away, step in and get closer. It is a great counter move.

Satan has entered and created pain and fear in your life, and your natural response is to pull away from God. I am begging you right here not to pull away, step in closer to God. Cry out to Him, and ask Him to deliver you from this moment. There is nothing haphazard about His plan. He is perfectly in control. You are in the midst of a storm, and my word for you is to chill! Relax. Don't fret. Do you know one of the most used phrases in the Bible is "Don't fret" or "Don't fear" or something similar? Do you know why? Because there are many times someone was afraid just like you, and they needed to hear those words. Do not be afraid, God is in control. He didn't fall asleep at the wheel of your life. You are going to be fine. He is planning His next miracle in your life just hoping you will trust Him. Don't give up on Him, He's never given up on you, and He isn't going to start.

I think it is safe to say the Spouse did not kill the bride in this story. Instead, He sacrificed His one and only Son to make you His bride. Let me remind you again, He didn't hold back to buy you. He gave His all. He didn't go cheap for you. He loves you so much, He waits (and has waited a long time) for you with arms open wide.

Maybe you are hurting right now. The sting is bad, the pain is deep. I promise you, I've been there. Stop reading the book right now and call out to Him. He is there for you. It doesn't have to be fancy or churchy. Just speak to your Father. In Romans 8:26 and 27 the scriptures say even when you can't find the words to say, the Holy Spirit is speaking to the Father on your behalf. Just cry out to Him. He loves you and not only does He hear you, He will answer and is waiting to be God. He will show you His might and glory as yet another testimony of what only He can do. This time, He wants to use *you* as the example.

He didn't kill His bride. He is innocent of all charges, but He is guilty of loving you in the first degree. Stop. Reach out to Him right now. We will wait . . .

AN ENEMY FROM THE OUTSIDE

So I think we made the case pretty convincing that the Groom did not kill His bride. If we are going to play this out as a responsible CSI agent, the next question always asked is, "Did the victim have any enemies?"

Let's begin with motive. Is there anyone who would want the bride of Christ dead? You don't have to look far. Maybe look at this morning's news or do an internet search on the word "Christian", and you will find that the bride has had enemies all throughout time.

I recently watched a few documentaries in preparation for a trip to Israel where I visited the holocaust museum. As I watched the movie *The Pianist* I was sickened to see what one talented and relatively "innocent" human being went through because of the flawed and demented philosophies of one man. How could one person stir up so much hatred throughout the world and lead us as the human race to commit such atrocities against mankind? As I visited the holocaust museum in Jerusalem, I walked slowly in disbelief at the unspeakable crimes committed against the nation of Israel. I kept asking myself, "Why would anyone go to such great lengths to destroy an entire race?" Adolph Hitler's goal was to destroy the past, present, and future of the Jewish nation. In the process of attempting to eliminate Israel's future, he ordered that around 1.5 million innocent *children* be murdered! I simply could not understand how a person could come to the conclusion that there was anything redemptive in what took place against the nation of Israel.

The lights came on though. How could someone (and it continues on to this day) hate a seemingly small, insignificant people group so much as to desire their extermination from the face of the planet? The answer is spiritual in nature. Where was salvation birthed? Israel. God, in the person of Jesus Christ, came to the earth and took on the form of human kind. He was born and lived for thirty-three years in the nation called Israel. Satan despises the very ground where the seed of salvation sprang forth. He seeks to destroy any evidence of the gift of Life and annihilate any evidence of God's love for mankind. He despises the nation of Israel and has gone to great lengths to wipe it off the face of the planet, because it is the very place where our salvation was birthed, purchased through murder, and sealed as Christ rose in victory. To this day the hatred continues against God's chosen people.

So, our salvation was born in Israel and that small nation has spread the good news of salvation and life abundant throughout the world. As a result it has an enemy and his name is Lucifer. Once an angel in the heavens, Lucifer was so overrun with pride that he decided he could be God and led a revolt, thereby earning expulsion from heaven along with about a third of the angels who joined with him.

Do you know you have the same enemy? I am not talking about just those who are called Christians. I am speaking to all my fellow human beings. If you have the capacity to fog a mirror you have that same enemy: Satan. Why you ask? The answer is very simple. You are made in the image of God and are designed to have fellowship with Him. In Genesis 1:26 God spoke forth and said, "Let us make man in our image." Satan hates God. He hates you because you were made in God's image. You cannot change that. God's indelible image is stamped upon you, and it absolutely ticks Satan off. It's true, you don't even have to be a Christian and Satan hates you.

Did you know that when you woke up this morning Satan had three things on his agenda for you? That's right; it is the same thing every day. Jesus revealed Satan's game plan in John 10:10. He seeks to steal from you, kill you, and destroy anything good in, about, or around you. You might think that if you are not a Christian you are off the hook so to speak. That's not true, you are a human. You were made to love God and follow Him. You were made in God's image.

Everything that God made Satan has a counterfeit for. God loves you; Satan hates you. He wants you dead, and he will go to any length, and take as much time as needed, because he is committed to doing what is in his nature to steal, kill and destroy. He wants to destroy you, to wipe your existence off the face of the world. To him, you are a filthy stench in his nostrils.

Many people get this concept completely backwards. They think God hates them, and Satan loves them. Satan promises "freedom", you can have whatever you want, and God only has a long list of rules to obey, making your life boring, right? You might have even believed that God hates you and wants to ruin your life. Do you know why you believed that? Because Satan is an expert liar. He has mastered the art of deceiving. He doesn't love you or care about you. Simply stated, he hates you and wants you dead.

One night I counseled a young man who was struggling to put the pieces together of what was in essence a really great life. He was a good looking, smart, and very gifted student athlete. As I tried to reason with him he muttered, "I wish they'd just shut up!"

In disbelief I responded, "I am sorry, did you just ask me to shut up?"

He looked up at me and said, "No, I wish *they* would shut up."

I asked him who *they* were, and he told me, "The voices".

I asked him, "What are the voices telling you?"

"They are saying there is no hope. I will never get out of this mess. They say that God hates me, that you hate me, and that there is no help for me. That I have gone too far."

It was then that I realized he was a victim of deception and lies. He had fallen prey to the master liar.

Can I ask you a question? Why is it so hard to believe the truth? Why is it so easy to believe a lie? You can't open God's word and read more than a few paragraphs before you are tripping all over God's love for you. The Psalms are very clear that God carefully crafted you in your mother's womb (Psalm 139:13). Yet as we walk through life, Satan's lies are lying around like landmines, telling you that you are rejected, hopeless, and worthless. He would like for you to believe that you are nothing more than dung in the bottom of the septic tank that nobody cares about. The Almighty says you are loved and your name is written on the palm of His hand (Isaiah 49:16). He loves you so much He would *die* for you. Yet Satan says God hates you, and you have no hope, and you choose to believe the lie. Why?

C.S. Lewis revealed in his book, *The Screwtape Letters*, that one of Satan's greatest tricks is to get us to believe he doesn't even exist. Yet all the while he lurks in the shadows lying and deceiving. It's not only the blood bought child of God he is hard at work to deceive, but all of mankind. He has mastered the art of selling the lie. He is great at it. Talk about your used car salesman!

Do you know what else? He doesn't care how long it takes. He will keep selling and selling, day after day, year after year. He will lie in wait for a lifetime. If need be, he'll wait right up until the grave. He keeps whispering lies to us and over time, we believe it and accept it as a part of our identity. James chapter 4 gives us the appropriate response to this tactic. Resist him and he will flee. The real issue for most of us is this, how much do we really resist? It seems like we just swallow the hook, line, and sinker without a fight. Know this too, the resistance James is talking about isn't passive. It is an active resistance.

It takes effort, thought, and persistence. It is a battle. However, if you are like me (and I fear many others), you find yourself at times giving into his lies and deceptions.

Did you know Satan has no authority over you? That's right. He has zero authority over you. He is a roaring lion, but Jesus put him in a cage many years ago. I remember reading a while back of a man who had his arm removed by a Bengal tiger at the zoo. It seems pretty obvious that they put dangerous and beastly animals in cages for a reason. If you are bold enough to stick your arm in the cage, then the tiger will just do what is in his nature. Scripture refers to Satan as a "roaring lion" (1 Peter 5:8), but if you keep your arms out of the cage, he cannot touch you. He has no right. He has no authority. You are a child of the Most High, so Satan must ask permission to do anything to you. All he can do is sit in his cage and roar threats and intimidations at you while swiping those big sharp claws against the bars of the cage. Yet through emotions like fear, worry, and anxiety he intimidates and does his best to nullify the plan God has for our life. We focus on the volume of his roar, the sharpness of his claws, and how thin the bars of the cage look. This is often why we hit a stage in life called the "midlife crisis" and say, "Wow, what a waste!" He creeps in and sells lies to us our whole life, and we finally give in to his plans. What a clever and, unfortunately, effective scheme.

I spoke to that young man that night at the table, and I told him he was being lied to. I pointed out how he had allowed Satan to come in through a portal in his life. He was a good kid raised in a pretty good Christian home where his mom and dad were in the ministry. He knew what God offered, but he just wanted to be cool. In that desire, he opened a door to the deceiver and said, "Okay, let me see what you got." Remind you of anything? Perhaps the Garden of Eden? Next thing he knew, he got a whole lot more than he bargained for, and he was a slave to sin in his life. He found out the hard way that Satan doesn't play fair and that he does play rough. He found out that Satan is a street brawler, and he will use whatever it takes to steal, kill, and destroy. He reached his arm in the cage of the lion, and he almost lost everything!

I prayed for that young man that night. I laid hands on his head and rebuked the deception and lies. I assisted him in getting the freedom that Jesus Christ offers. I am glad to say that young man is currently studying to go into the ministry. That night his life changed. He had a truth encounter and truth won.

The truth counters the lies. The truth marches on. It prevails. Like a candle in the darkness, once it is lit, the darkness has to yield to it, because the darkness cannot consume the light.

My pastor so faithfully shares this point over and over again in his teaching. When you see theft, death, and destruction, it is *not* a sign that God is out to get you; it is proof that you have an enemy! That is evidence that you have an enemy and he has been busy doing what is in his nature all up in your life. I think it is messed up and clever at the same time. In the midst of all of this, we don't see the truth that the enemy is at work. Instead, as we discussed in the last chapter, we often blame God. We think that our Father in heaven is the boy with the magnifying glass, and we are the ants on the anthill. What a demented and completely opposite view of God as personally handcrafted by the liar, Satan, himself.

Please be certain to dial in to the truth of the matter, because the truth sets you free (John 8:32). God loves you, and because of that great love He offers you life, true freedom, and abundance. His name is Wonderful, Counselor, the Everlasting, full of grace and *truth*.

For years I have heard people ask questions along the lines of, "Do I have to go to church to be a Christian?" Or perhaps the other one is, "Do I have to read the Bible?" I guess the thought is to get away with as little as possible and still get into heaven. Let me attempt to put a different perspective on it. Have I mentioned you have an enemy that is constantly at work to destroy you? I think you do have to go to church, read your Bible, and also attend small groups. I'd recommend this and the other basic disciplines of the Christian faith to know the truth about God and the truth about the one who seeks to destroy you.

One Sunday I met a young man in church. As we talked, he began to share with me that he wasn't the good guy I thought he was. He told me he had recently come to church, because he had done something that cost him his job. As a result, his life began a downward spiral. He began to pour out his life, and the tears ran down his face amidst a crowd of folks. As this young man was pouring his heart out to me, I felt the Holy Spirit speak to me, reminding me of something I had heard that was profound and life-changing.

I interrupted him and asked, "Do you know the difference between conviction and condemnation?" He said he didn't. I explained to him, "You just told me what you did, but you said it as if that was who you are. Condemnation says you are a loser and a screw up who lost his job because of poor choices. Conviction says you are not living up to the calling of your life. You are not living your destiny. Condemnation is a tool of the enemy to tie your sins to your identity, and it leads to death. Conviction is a gift of the Holy Spirit that says you are a son of the Most High, and you are not living out your destiny and that leads to brokenness, repentance, and ultimately restoration and life. Condemnation is a tool of the devil, and it leads to death. Conviction is of the Holy Spirit, and it leads to restoration and life. The Holy Spirit spoke to me as you were talking and told me to tell you that your sin is not who you are. It is only what you did, and there is forgiveness for what you did. Stop listening to the lies of the enemy and receive truth, you are a loved and forgiven son of the Most High. You are a mighty warrior."

He looked at me through the tears and said he had never heard that before. He, too, had a truth encounter, and the truth prevailed. Presently he is in church and growing and overcoming the past and his mistakes.

For those of you who are children of the Most High, do you realize He has called you to do this kind of ministry? In Luke 4:18-19 Jesus revealed His ministry objectives. He passed that same ministry on to us.

> "THE SPIRIT OF THE LORD IS UPON ME,
> BECAUSE HE ANOINTED ME TO PREACH THE
> GOSPEL TO THE POOR.
> HE HAS SENT ME TO PROCLAIM RELEASE TO THE
> CAPTIVES,
> AND RECOVERY OF SIGHT TO THE BLIND,
> TO SET FREE THOSE WHO ARE OPPRESSED,
> TO PROCLAIM THE FAVORABLE YEAR OF THE
> LORD."

Here Jesus reveals that He is anointed by the Holy Spirit to:

1. Preach good news to the poor and thereby offer hope.
2. Proclaim the release of those stuck in bondage.
3. Help those blinded by lies to see things the way they really are, in other words the truth.
4. Set free those who are oppressed or weighed down by life's burdens.
5. Proclaim the favor of the Lord. God loves you and His favor is upon you.

Do you know that is the ministry God has called you to? Do you know that those are the words you are to speak into others' lives to counteract the lies the enemy has been feeding them for a lifetime? Do you know that this is nothing more than the mingling of the prophetic and encouraging gifts? All too often I have been guilty of, and have observed others, using the enemy to drive a person's sins deeper into their skulls in an attempt to bring about repentance, to be the Roman Soldiers and crucify these souls and make certain they are aware of their sins.

Here in Colorado we have a saying, "If you don't like the weather, just wait a minute." We've had snowstorms as late as April and May with 60 inches of snow in a couple days time. On one of these occasions, a man I know was called by his son to come to school to pick him up. As he approached an intersection, a vehicle slid out of control and ran into a pile of snow. The man jumped out of his car, as did another man, and approached the stranded vehicle. The other gentleman began to lecture the driver on her winter driving habits. My friend looked at him and said, "Hey, how about we just push her out so she can get on her way?" She obviously wasn't getting out of the snow bank via lecture. It took someone to help her get unstuck.

How true this is for the body of Christ. Many of us feel called to the ministry of lecture. We are very gifted at the little known, and even less appreciated, gift of being judgmental. We often feel compelled to share our wealth of spiritual perfection to tell people how they shouldn't have gotten stuck in the first place and that they should be more like us. Truth be told, they are stuck, and they don't like it. They just need us to give them a push and get them on their way again. How often we are used of the enemy to further discourage and drive hurting ones away from healing and victory. But I digress . . .

We are called to a ministry of reconciliation that takes our God-given spiritual gifts and uses them to dispel the lies of the enemy with the truth of scripture, humbly considering ourselves, because we too could fall into the same temptation and sin (Galatians 6:1).

Satan has enough help on his side of the fence. The Kingdom of God doesn't need sinners pretending to be flawless, operating out of arrogance and joining forces with Satan to heap condemnation on fellow fallen saints. Jesus addressed this issue when the woman caught in adultery was dragged before him. The Pharisees wanted to trip Jesus up by saying that the law stated she should be stoned. Jesus' response echoes throughout eternity, "Anyone here who is free from all sin, you be the first to throw a stone at her." He knew that all have sinned and fallen short of the mark of perfection as stated by God.

He said that sin is sin. It doesn't matter which sin, all sin separates you from God.

We also know that Jesus only did what He saw His Father do (John 5:19). He offered gracious correction in humility that changed her life. So we too ought to emulate Christ when it comes to our judgment habits. We all have sinned (Romans 3:23) that means you need to put your rock down. Just set it down right there on the ground. You won't need it. You are not qualified, and just like me, you have sinned. Your sin is not better than someone else's sin, the only difference is it is the sin you struggle with.

It is easy to see the shortcomings of others and think they are bad, evil, and wrong. I think another tactic of the enemy is to wound and ultimately divide the body of Christ. The point is that we are all fallen, broken sinners in need of a Savior. Let's let the Savior be the Savior and focus on our own areas of growth.

So we have a dead bride on the couch. We have done some investigation, and we have found that there is one who has motive. Satan, the liar, is certainly the enemy of the bride of Christ. He certainly had motive to steal, kill, and destroy, however, I have some bad news for you. As we look this scene over, we cannot find evidence that this bride was in fact murdered by the outside enemy. We cannot take this before the judge and place this on the altar of evidence and get a fully guilty verdict. If we are going to get to the bottom of this and get real answers, we have to broaden our investigation.

OVERCOME BY SICKNESS

Is it possible that the enemy of this bride used some type of weapon that was more than a simple murder weapon? Could he have used some type of biological weaponry? Is it possible that the bride was poisoned little by little, day after day, or made ill by some airborne pathogen?

The case can be made that she lived in a world that was full of sickness and that she existed in a culture laden with every type of disease. It would be easy to point at an obvious enemy, however in the name of good CSI work, we need to look at all the facts and form a solid conclusion. If we are going to be objective, the facts could just as easily point to the reality that the bride had gotten sick and died.

It is obvious that we live in a very broken world. It doesn't take but a simple look at a news channel, a glance through the newspaper, or a quick search engine peek to find the extreme sickness of our broken culture. Everywhere we look we see children molested, school shootings, divorce, hatred, murder, and the list goes on and on. You do not have to be a puritan, prude, or pessimist to deduce that mankind is not doing so well as a society. Still, I am often taken aback, at the surprised looks on people's faces when I mention things that follow in this chapter.

In his book *The Knowledge of the Holy*, A.W. Tozer mentions that we have entertained a lesser view of God and a thousand lesser evils have followed. That was written in 1941. We have entertained such a low view of God that we have no clue of His character, majesty, and the amazing plan He has put together for us.

I was once speaking at a youth function in Chicago. A friend of mine said that he wanted me to travel with him and speak, but he had one stipulation: I was not allowed to use notes. I thought, *"Wow, how stupid! What am I supposed to do, wing it? Shall I use old memorized material?"*

When my flight landed in O'Hare that Thursday night, I was picked up by my friend, and we met with the youth staff of the church that night. We just asked generic questions like "What work is God doing here and what things are you struggling with?" Then we turned in for the night. We fasted from food the next day before the youth event and sought the Holy Spirit's lead on what to do. My friend invited a worship leader, prayer warriors, and me, and they were all as thrown to the planning wolves as I was. My friend said my time of preparation was to sit and wait to hear what to say from the Holy Spirit. My job was easy, just listen and be obedient to say what the Spirit told me to say. To which I said, "Yeah . . . right!"

I found myself sitting on an asphalt parking lot in Chicago against the basketball hoop asking God (utilizing my spiritual gift of sarcasm), "So, what do you want me to say to these nice people tonight?" I guess I wasn't sure what I would hear or if I would hear anything at all. What the Holy Spirit delivered wasn't what I would have said. I found myself in a tough situation. Only hours from speaking to a group of total strangers, and good church-going people nonetheless, God said, "Tell them they do not know me." I was like, *"Yeah right God, really? You want me to go tell these kids they don't know You? Of course they know You! Most of them have been on a mission trip. Maybe you aren't aware of this God but this is a discipleship weekend, not an outreach."* I tried to assemble a message that would fit the occasion that afternoon, but it was like I had a "preacher's block" and nothing seemed to flow for me. Nothing seemed to work. I was frustrated and confused, and truthfully, I was not sure what to think. I didn't have my usual library of books and notes to dig through. Later that night, I stood nervously before that group of teenagers feeling extremely unprepared and found myself saying the unthinkable. The message went something like this:

"Umm, I was out in your parking lot earlier asking God what He wanted to say to you today. I listened really hard and thought about this a lot. I wanted to make sure it was right and after much searching and struggling He told me to tell you that 'you do not know Him.'" I felt something rising up in me as I spoke the words. I didn't really know what would come out of my mouth next, but I continued and the words began to flow. I said, "He told me to tell you that if you reverse the letters of His name," I found a dry erase marker and a board to write on, "you spell 'dog'. God is saying that many of you treat him like you do your dog. Instead of you being humble before Him and at His service, He is just there for you. He is only there for your protection, for your entertainment, maybe for companionship or to turn tricks for you. He further asks what is worse than me implying it is you are actually doing it." A handful of kids got up from the room and left! I was like, "*See God, I told you that wouldn't fly well.*" Despite the feeling of confrontation and even failure, I continued. What else could I do, I had no notes. I might as well have tried singing the national anthem in French, backwards, but I continued, "God says that you have created a God of your own thinking. You have drawn a picture of God, and it looks a lot like Him, it seems to be Him, but it is not. It is an idol. It is a dead idol. It has no life. It will not give you victory over sin. You will not have power, because He is God and your hand drawn idol is not. It is dead, worthless, and you are committing idolatry."

I spoke on that theme for about 30 minutes. The youth attending just stared at me with shock on their faces. My friend stood up at the end of my message and started to debrief what was said and what had happened in the room. He was asking the kids what they heard God saying to them. After a few minutes the kids that had left returned. I couldn't blame them for leaving. I felt like I'd punched them in the mouths, however when they came through the door their faces were tear-soaked and smudged. My friend welcomed them back and asked them why they left the room. They said as I spoke the Holy Spirit came down on them in a very powerful way, like nothing they had experienced before, and began to convict them about what was being said.

One young man said, "When Mark said I was treating God like my dog that hit me really hard. I got up, went into the sanctuary, and fell on the floor at the altar and cried out to God. I was confessing sin and repenting before God. I couldn't believe I treated Him that way." The others shared his conviction and relayed similar stories.

God did something powerful that night. Why do I share it with you? Because the concept A.W. Tozer was referring to has not only been happening since his time, it has gone far beyond an epidemic in the church today. The world and its business practices, along with man-made ideology, has crept into the church and invaded our minds with garbage that is absolutely unfitting of the Almighty. Our thoughts of God are so low they are unfit for His ears. Our beloved brother Tozer says it this way:

> *"What comes into our minds when we think about God is the most important thing about us. The history of mankind will show that no people has ever risen above its religion, and man's spiritual history will positively demonstrate that no religion has ever been greater than it's idea of God. Worship is pure or base as the worshipper entertains high or low thoughts of God."*[1]

Why do I bring this up at this point in the book? Simply stated, we have drifted so off base in our understanding of who God is that we have adopted a breed of Christianity that is nothing like what God intended it to be. It is either laced with liberalism where everything, anything, and nothing is God or inundated with legalism, where nothing is holy enough, and no one will ever measure up. It is spiritual malnutrition to the highest degree. Neither extreme is helpful, and they both lead to death.

We as Americans (generally speaking) have access to some of the finest food in the world. We have access to as much of the food as we want. We have access to the best health care and fitness clubs. Yet we are a sickly bunch. As a matter of fact, we have the highest medical bills of any country in the world. We have hospitals full of heart attack victims, cancer patients, and a whole host of other diseases. It would almost seem as if we are inventing diseases on a daily basis. Let me ask you: was your grandfather or great grandfather gluten intolerant? Did he have to have his prostate carved out? Did his father have ADD or ADHD? Where did all this stuff come from?

It has been well documented that our soils are depleted of the essential nutrients that we need to remain healthy. This was a problem years ago, and it has only become worse as we see an increase of pesticides and chemical fertilizers. It has gotten to a point where our food is actually depleted of the required nutrients. So if you were to go to the grocery store and buy only vegetables and eat as a vegetarian, you will still be missing the necessary nutrients that your body needs to remain vibrant and healthy. We have such a poor diet that even though we eat loads of food, our bodies are starving. We are starving even as we eat our veggies!

We aren't even talking about the junk food junkies who live on snack cakes and soft drinks. Because of the lack of proper nutrition, our digestive system itself has become depleted and cannot properly process our food. It is damaged and cannot function properly. This is what doctors call "leaky gut syndrome." The digestive system is so damaged that even if you eat perfectly and have good food, you still cannot absorb the minerals and nutrients in the quantities needed. Your body could only grab a few things to maintain life and not thrive.

As this process goes on and on, the body becomes further broken and damaged and disease takes over.

Guess what? I just described to you the condition the bride suffers from today. We have suffered from spiritual malnutrition, be it liberalism or legalism. We have become sickly and are in bad shape. We have rampant disease in the body of Christ, and it is like we are inventing more diseases every day.

It has been said that now the divorce rate is higher in the church than in the world. Did you know that by age 40 over 40% of Christian marriages (yes, in the church) will experience adultery firsthand? Did you know that in many cases it isn't the husband doing the deed, but the wife? While men across this country filled football stadiums at Promise Keepers events, making promises to remain faithful and become better men, the attack was directed at their brides. There is that enemy at work again to spread the killing, stealing, and destruction.

Did you know that most young people in our youth ministries never take their virginity to the altar of marriage? Wasn't it just a decade ago youth pastors and teens alike were signing pledge cards to "wait"? At that event there were so many pledge cards they stacked them from the floor of a football stadium to the roof?

Have you heard the one about the young girls that are sold into prostitution at age twelve? They perform tricks for men as sex slaves, and their pimps make millions of dollars a year. You've heard about this taking place in Cambodia, but I'm talking about where the problem is at a feverish epidemic: America. Right here in your country, your state, your city, yes, right in your neighborhood. The days of littering, talking in class and petty dime store theft being of chief concern are gone. Now our sons and daughters are being treated like trash. The pollution problem has grown far beyond the trash rolling down the street, it has filtered into our homes, and we are sick, weak, and dying. We just don't know it.

Or do we? I'd like to think that we have somehow gotten really busy in our fast-paced society and just didn't see this creeping up on us. But perhaps some of us are guilty of turning a blind eye or perhaps we are so full of ourselves that we just don't bother to take a look around. There is so much more that I am not discussing. What about abortion? What about the problem of homelessness, poverty, alcoholism, drug addiction, and teen pregnancy? The list goes on and on. Nonetheless, to put it in the farmer's term, we are in deep manure!

We have grown so sickly and weak, our doctrine is so pathetic, our view of God so impoverished and needy that we are dying and disease laden, yet we do not know it! Week after week we gather in our places of worship and sing, and we hear a comforting message, and let's face it, we hide behind our masks and stain glass and are not living out our destiny and calling. We have lost track of who we are and what we have been called to. We have been lured into a foggy slumber, and the price tag is staggering.

I had an experience once in the hospital that is forever etched in my mind. Quite some time ago I had a fairly simple procedure that was supposed to be outpatient. I was to go in early that morning and come out in the afternoon to go home and rest peacefully. Only, it didn't quite go that way. I went in and had the procedure and found out that I have a reaction to anesthesia that causes me to sleep very deeply, unable to wake up. As I laid in recovery after the surgery, I found myself so weak I could not even open my eyes. I could hear the nurse telling me I had to open my eyes so I could go back to my room. I could hear what was going on, but I could not open my eyes. I could not breathe very deeply and felt as if I was getting sick. I began to move my head back and forth, side to side. I was still so weak I could not open my eyes. I began to upset the nurse because I was moving my head. I felt as if I was suffocating, and I began to panic. I tried to talk but was too hoarse and too weak to utter the words. I smelled the horrible smell in the oxygen mask of ether and bad breath, and it smelled as if I was re-breathing my own disgusting used air. I tried to get the mask off my face, only to frustrate my nurse even more. Finally

I vomited. The nurse removed the mask from my face, and I gasped. Just then I heard another nurse exclaim, "You idiot! You didn't turn it on!" I was suffocating and too weak to do anything about it. This is the condition of the bride. She is weak and powerless to even awaken, and she is badly in need of help.

I understand the sickness in the world is partly the work of the enemy. He is committed to his craft and works feverishly spreading trash in the world, however we the church were left to do the work of ministry. We somehow got off course. We spent decades arguing among ourselves about everything from our naval, the rapture, hymns versus choruses, and eternal security while the devil laughed his butt off. In the meantime, abortion became legal, evolution became fact, living together became a way of life, and the divorce rate in the church became higher than in the world. Hell is getting pretty crowded, the homeless starve, young girls are sold as sex slaves, and the church has become irrelevant.

There is a great deal of sickness and trash in the world we live in and much of it was deposited here by the enemy and his workers, and unfortunately, it was on our watch. Again, the price tag is beyond high. It is staggering, and it has to break the heart of the Groom, Christ, to see the state of affairs of the world He died to redeem. Remember, He was murdered for this!

One might make the case that we didn't mean to. One might say we really didn't want it to be this way. This reminds me of a little issue my wife had with me when we were on vacation a few years back. We were on a trip in the beautiful mountains of Colorado. We went to Glenwood Springs where they have a small amusement park on the top of one of the mountains. You have to take a gondola ride to the top to enjoy the fun. After a long fun-filled day of rides and laughs, we went back to the gondola to head down to our hotel. It was hot, the line was long, and everyone just wanted to get down the mountain. Tensions were a little high as we waited in line. I stepped back on one occasion to talk to my wife and stepped on her foot. She let out a painful sigh, and I got "the look"! Maybe you have had "the look" too? I immediately responded, "But I didn't mean to step on you!" For whatever reason this didn't seem to matter to her, and she said something very profound in that moment that I think applies here, "Well, it still hurt!"

The fact that the church is dead and has become irrelevant in a hurting and needy world doesn't change because "we didn't mean to". This is serious stuff. In trying to remedy the situation of mankind's sinful condition, God didn't approach the situation with anything less than His very best! He gave His one and only precious Son. That's how important the situation is, and we dare not take a casual approach. We have got to awaken from the fog and see how precious every single soul is to Him. Unless we have been misinformed, there is not one single insignificant soul in the eyes of God. Never has been and never will be.

So, have you heard we live in a broken world? Throughout the centuries the bride of Christ has not influenced the world, but instead been influenced by the world. Day by day she has left her post. She has not tended her garden, and the result is an overgrown mess of weeds! Have you ever stopped to think about what happens when you leave soil to itself? A farm field left abandoned does not produce beautiful flowers, fruits, and vegetables; it produces weeds. We have not been about doing the things of God, we have not stayed awake, and we have allowed the culture to dictate to us the rules of engagement.

For years the church has not spoken at all about matters that we should have been vocal on, and we have inherited a mess. We have allowed society to creep into the church and dictate to us our heritage, our culture, and our destiny. If the church does not speak on important issues, the world speaks and sets the default in our silence. By not speaking out and being heard in a loving and firm manner, the world spoke on our behalf and gave us broken, defunct, and anemic views on far too many issues, and there is a price to pay now. We ignored our calling to speak out, and it is biting us in the proverbial rear end.

Again, we wonder how God could let this happen. Let me say it, we have found the enemy, and he is us!

I want to share another gruesome piece of this puzzle in something that I observed with my own eyes recently. I mentioned that I visited the Holocaust museum in Jerusalem. Before we left the bus, our tour guide warned us when we got into the museum, as Americans and as Christians, we might find some of their observations and deductions offensive. I thought, *Well of course. We are Americans, and we are Christians on top of that! Breathing offends us!* When I entered the museum it didn't take me long to understand what our guide was referring to. Right there before my eyes I saw actual letters to our United States Congress encouraging them to forbid Jewish refugees entrance to our country. I saw political cartoons with the statue of liberty turning her back on tens of thousands of Jews who were homeless. I heard stories of churches that, by and large, remained silent and turned a blind eye to the plight of the Jews. Their opinion was "It's not my problem". I will pause here and say, there were many who helped, and they deserve the blessings of heaven, and they are appreciated by the nation of Israel and even have a space in the museum dedicated to their efforts. But by and large, American Christians were deaf and blind to the needs of the Jews and millions were slaughtered as a result.

This reminds me of our country today. Does the church know that tonight young teenage girls that have been taken as sex slaves perform unthinkable sexual favors in truck stops by night? I thought we fought a civil war to free people from slavery. Do you even have a clue how out of control and how huge the problem is and how it continues to grow? I encourage you to put the book down and go do an internet search on human trafficking. Bring a barf bag with you. Go to a chat room and look for discussions on the topic. Look at the amount of people who encourage it, who think it is funny and who joke about it.

Does the church see the problem of homelessness or is that someone else's problem? Does the church feel the compulsion to remain silent on matters that tear at the heart of God? Is the church more concerned about the millions of innocent children slaughtered in abortion clinics in the name of convenience and choice or about the balance of its 401k? Seriously?

Are you still thinking the bride is alive? Do you think she is living her destiny as the blood bought virgin saving herself for her husband's return?

Do we realize that over 90% of the young people that go through our youth groups will walk across our platforms at high school graduation and keep walking right out the doors and never come back to church again? Why is that? Maybe because there is no life in our churches, and there is no reason to attend church, because we have tried to compete with the world for so long that there is no essence of the Holy Spirit of God in our midst. We have become just like the world, and there is little to no difference. I don't blame these kids. Why attend? Why bother? We drive by the parks, lakes, and ski slopes on our way to church, and they are full of people who don't come to church. Why would they? There is nothing there. It is more refreshing to breathe the fresh air than to comb through the carpets trying to find a few left-over crumbs of the Bread of Life from ancient revivals, yet we blame *them* and think it is *their* fault.

How much longer will we allow the world to spin out of control and sit back and lament how bad the world is getting? How bad will it have to get before *you* will do something about it? How many homeless people will you pass by? How many more abortions have to happen, how many divorces, how much longer will the sickness and disease spread before we fall to our knees in brokenness and say "God I have had enough!" It has been said many times before and rings true today, perhaps the reason God has not visited us with revival is because we are so content to live without it.

I recently heard of a pastor in Loveland, Colorado who did something that literally brought me to tears. Pastor Jonathan Wiggans was fairly new to his post at Resurrection Fellowship Church. The former pastor had served that church and community for over thirty years. This guy was in deep weeds the day he walked in the door. He didn't ask for something to make his new job more difficult. I imagine he wanted a nice, smooth transition into this new position at this large church. Not making waves is the common approach of the new pastor.

He was notified by a member of his church about a brewing controversy in the community and was asked how the church would get involved in the Loveland Art Museum over the piece of art entitled "The Misadventures of The Romantic Cannibals". The Pastor began to investigate the piece of art and was left with only one option in his mind. He cried out to God and asked for guidance. What ensued is one of the only examples that I am aware of where the church had a profoundly positive influence on her community over a controversial subject.

Pastor Wiggans found the email address of the author of the piece of art in the midst of the controversy and asked a simple question. He asked the artist to describe to him what he was attempting to say through his art. By this time the artist had received thousands of hate mail letters and death threats from Christians. One was so bold as to say that he ought to climb into a bath tub and slit his wrists as his days were numbered. To Pastor Wiggans' surprise, the artist, Enrique Chagoya, replied to his email within hours. He was surprised and felt blessed at the loving response of the pastor in the midst of all of the hatred.

Mr. Chagoya went on to describe that his painting was an attempt to display what the church had done to Christ, the beautiful and unspotted Son of God. He described that his piece of art was intended to show how those in leadership had defiled and desecrated the pure, undefiled Christ and used Him for their own profit and advancement.

I will save you the many details of what transpired from that point. The entire story can be observed by going to the church website (www.rez.org) and clicking on the story *Tougher Than Nails*. The pastor reached out in Christ's love to Mr. Chagoya and sought to first understand him. He offered to hear Mr. Chagoya's heart instead of seeking to judge and condemn it, and the result was yet another truth encounter.

The pastor invited Mr. Chagoya to do another painting of Jesus, one that depicted Jesus' character and true nature rather than that of the fallen ones who had desecrated Him; he even offered to hang it in his church. What was an ugly and evil day being stirred by the hatred of hell ended up becoming a beautiful story of the bride of Christ ministering to her community.

We were commissioned and commanded to go out and be the church, to make disciples of the nations, and somehow we got off course. The situation is serious, the consequences horrific, and God hasn't lost track of our effort. He has not given up and neither should we. We have much to do, and, rather than continue to discuss how bad the world is, let's focus on one other potential way the bride has died. I think you might be surprised.

As in the last chapter, it would be easy to end this one saying it is the fault of the world. The sickness of this diseased culture has overtaken us. But no, I am sorry, I cannot let that go. That is an excuse. That is a cheap cop out. We cannot blame the devil nor can we blame the world that surrounds us. We must push further into the matter and come to the truth, and the guilty party must be exposed.

Notes:

[1]   Aiden Wilson Tozer, The Knowledge of the Holy. Harper and Brothers Publishers, New York, 1961, P.9.

SELF-INFLICTED GUNSHOT WOUND

We have gone through the normal suspects in our attempt to find the killer of the bride of Christ. We sought the spouse first. We came to the conclusion that the Loving God would never kill His own bride, because He already sacrificed His one and only Son for her. We looked at her biggest enemy, Satan. He certainly has a role in the matter, but we deduced he is just an accomplice. We looked at the culture she lived in and discovered brokenness, sickness, and disease. Again, there is a case to be made that the surroundings were bad, but there is not clear, conclusive evidence that she died from the influence of the world. I think there is one more possibility.

I am tired of the lack of authenticity in the church today. People go to church week after week, bleeding out yet when you ask them "How's it going?" you get the answer of "Fine! How about you?"

This reminds me of one Wednesday night when I was a youth pastor. I was in a hurry to get to the youth and get the evening started when I ran past a friend in the hallway and said, "Hey man! How's it going?"

He looked back at me and said in a soft voice, "Oh, fine. Everything's fine."

Away we went. But in an instant the Holy Spirit stopped me and said, "Ask him again." I stopped and called him by name. He stopped and turned around and looked at me. I said, "No really, how is it going?"

He looked at the floor for a second and paused before looking back up at me with tears in his eyes. "It's not good Pastor Mark, not good at all."

As we spoke I realized there was hurt deep, deep down inside. We talked and decided to get together for breakfast. When we met, there were several hurts that came out, and the situation was pretty serious. The enemy had gotten into his family and was doing what he does: killing, stealing, and destroying.

Why do we hide? Is it shame? Why do we fear looking bad to one another? What have we turned church into anyhow? The way I see it, church ought to be an emergency room, a place where people go who are hurting, broken, sick, and dying to find rest for their souls and healing for their wounds.

I once had a guy who did not know Christ tell me he refused to go to church, because it was full of hypocrites. He then went on to tell me about how he visited church once and sort of liked it. He went with his wife a few times and started to get into it. They went for a while, but he decided to stop going. His wife left him for another woman in that church. The enemy comes to steal, kill, and destroy. You can only imagine the black eye the bride of Christ got on that one in that man's opinion.

My response to him was of great pain and sympathy. I apologized to him for the horrible experience the people of the Christian community gave him. I went on to say this as well, "You know though I am not so surprised." He was shocked. He began to look more intently at me and asked if this happens a lot in the church I attend.

I responded to his question with a question. I asked him, "Would you be surprised and angered if you went down to the emergency room of the local hospital and found people there who were in pain, bleeding all over the place? Would you be shocked if people were throwing up all over, cussing at doctors and nurses, and yelling in their pain?" He said no, not at all. I asked him then why would he be surprised that this type of thing happens at church? A church should be nothing more than an emergency room for spiritually hurting people. People come to church that are broken. When they get there, there are fallen people attending who are doing their best to minister God's healing power to them. All the while there is an enemy who is trying to destroy their work: stealing medicine, spilling things, and turning off the electricity.

Back to our last potential scenario for the murder of the bride of Christ; follow along on the 911 call:

911: 911 ... What is your emergency?

Caller: I have been shot! I am bleeding, help ...

911: Are you alone?

Caller: Yes!

911: What is your address?

Caller: 1234 Main Street

911: Are you seriously hurt?

Caller: Yes, I am bleeding, and I don't think I am going to be able to stay conscious much longer ...

911: Okay, did you see the shooter?

Caller: Yes, yes I did.

911: What did the shooter look like?

Caller: A lot like me.

911: (Pause) Okay, can you give me more information. How tall was the shooter, where did the shooter go?

Caller: (Pause) well, the shooter is still here . . .

911: (urgent voice) I thought you said you were all alone!

Caller: I am! I am the shooter. I shot myself!

You see, we can look at the things of God, and we can believe the lies that Satan has fed us. We can believe that God doesn't love us, and we can believe that God has wounded us. We can look at the war that Satan has assaulted us with and blame him for the dead. We can look at the culture around us and blame its broken sick condition and say we have been infected. When in reality, we are dead because, well, we did this to ourselves.

It was suicide! A self-inflicted gunshot wound!

Stop for a second and process that thought. Just stop, put the book down, and before you read any further, try and process how we have done this to ourselves.

For years I believed that as a minister of the gospel, a husband, and a father, I was largely ineffective. I was frustrated and angry at God. I was running around looking for Satan, and everything that went wrong I blamed on him. I looked at the moral decay all around me and blamed the world for my lack of growth and the death and destruction. No doubt, the enemy and the world created some part of the mess. But If I am to be honest, it's my own darn fault!

I asked Jesus to be my Savior at age five, and I grew up in the church. I went to a good Bible college and attended and pastored in good churches. I am an ordained minister and attended all the conferences and crusades. Yet I felt that all along my ministry was ineffective, because I was operating in my flesh and not walking in the Spirit. Here is where I think it gets pretty edgy. I anticipate a good amount of negative feedback on what I am about to say. This runs the risk of sounding uncaring and I really don't mean to come off that way but I really don't care about popular opinion because I feel it needs to be said.

We have castrated the trinity! Yep, I said it, we have castrated the trinity. We do not have a trinity in the body of Christ outside the ancient creeds and hymnals. We have a duo. We teach and preach about the Father and His great love in sending His Son. We talk about Jesus, His ministry on earth, and His great love for mankind and amazing sacrifice in dying on the cross for us. Please do not get me wrong. I agree with all that I just said, God's love and Jesus love . . . absolutely amazing! There's nothing like it, unbelievable and certainly transformational. We need to teach about the Father and Jesus. We need to preach about them all we can. Where the church has fallen short is in the teaching of the other third of the trinity, our life-giving source of true power, the Holy Spirit.

The term castration sounds crass and gruff yet when you think about it, what we have done is eliminate our ability to reproduce the true power and life of the Holy Spirit of the scriptures. I have heard (and said) so many times that I want to be like the church in Acts chapter 2. I want to see thousands added to our numbers daily. I want to be like the apostle Peter and stand in front of my toughest critics and preach a very powerful and confrontational message and see them cut to the heart and break in repentance. What happened to that church just before that powerful message was preached? They waited on God. They sought God and did nothing until they were anointed and empowered by the Holy Spirit. After they were anointed by the Holy Spirit, then ministry took place, then He added to their number thousands of converts. They were told to go to the upper room and wait.

What would have happened if they had run out to do ministry? They more than likely would have fallen flat on their faces in frustration. Look at the example of Christ Himself. He did not move into works of ministry until after His baptism. Do you remember what happened then? The Holy Spirit descended on Him in the form of a dove. Jesus didn't even attempt ministry without the Spirit's power.

I have a pretty good idea of what happened to the modern church and how we got to where we are. I went to a good Bible college, heard enough seminars on building the "successful church" to gag an entire herd of cattle, and listened to piles of lectures on how to reach the lost. In all of the trainings, I heard all about the Father and the Son and their great work. Their works are great, but what about the rest of the story? What about the life-giving power of the Holy Spirit?

Again there is an enemy at work here. Here is how I think the story played out. Years ago the enemy sat down with his thugs, and they wanted to devise a plan to hinder the effectiveness of the church and throw a monkey wrench in the machine called the new testament church. Some lower-ranking, flunky demon came up with the idea of getting us to fight about something. After all, we are humans. We will fight over pretty much anything. So somehow during the conversation someone brought up the great idea about fighting over spiritual gifts. Then a legitimate question came up, "How can we make them fight over something so precious and beneficial? After all, they are gifts from God to His beloved bride." Then someone came up with extremes and abuses, and the conversation went off like a nuclear bomb.

We have taken the beautiful gifts of God and blown them in excess and no longer seek the Giver of the gift, just the gifts. We went to extremes and abused the gifts of God; we used the gifts for ourselves instead of His glory and His body. Some people did goofy things in their flesh and called them gifts of God. There were phonies, frauds, and flakes tossing around the precious gifts of God like cheap toys, using them for their own gain. Then we had people take sides; we had others take shots and others that took a stab at trying sort it out. Some had to part fellowship with them, and denominations began to spring up, and the gifts were branded to certain radicals and denominations and it got pretty messy from there. To protect us all from ourselves we had to stop talking about the Holy Spirit and the gifts of the Spirit so we could sit down and have a cup of Joe without getting into a fight and parting fellowship. Perhaps you think it silly, I agree, however I think that today Satan is lying in the fetal position laughing at us, pausing only to say, "Watch them try to do this in their flesh!"

In the early days of my ministry I was taught to stay away from anything that looked charismatic, and truthfully I wanted to, because it looked pretty weird indeed. There were those who meant well and loved me and wanted to protect me from false doctrines and phonies. They told me to stay away from it all, because it is a slippery slope, and you will be shipwrecked. There were certain types and certain denominations we just needed to stay away from. Because of abuses, they had a legitimate point.

I will never forget going to church with a friend from work. I had suffered a fractured arm earlier that week and was wearing an obvious, large, fresh white cast to protect the injury. When I entered the church, I was greeted by the pastor who looked down at my obviously messed up arm. We spoke for a few seconds and moved into the sanctuary to be seated. The service started, the worship was uplifting, and I was blessed to be there. When the pastor got up to speak he began to get words of revelation, knowledge, and prophecy. He began to dance on the stage and speak in a language I didn't understand. Then he paused briefly to let everyone know that the Holy Spirit had just spoken to him, and there was a young man in the church that had a broken arm. He said this as he looked right at me and offered to heal my arm. Needless to say, I picked my stuff up and left immediately. My friend followed me out and apologized for the scam. I felt like I needed to take a shower.

There are multiple books written about the abuses of the gifts and why we as "good sound Christians" need to stay away from it all. I have even heard respected and gifted Bible teachers of very prominent ministries refer to the gifts of the Spirit (more particularly healings and tongues) as "doctrines of demons" and warned anyone participating in them that they are doing the work of the devil. Even though I wanted to stay away from heresy, something didn't sit right. I felt then that these teachers were skating on thin ice on a hot day.

The teaching I am referring to is called cessationism. It is the belief that the gifts of the Spirit at some point and time ceased (thus cessationism) and are no longer necessary.

I grew up in a conservative denomination that attempted to strike a middle ground on the sign gifts (healing, speaking in tongues, and other miracles) or gifting of the Spirit. This denomination taught "Seek not, forbid not" on the gifts of tongues and that the other sign gifts were relevant for today's church, however in over fifteen years of growing up in that denomination, and nearly eight years of serving in that denomination as an ordained minister, never did I hear anyone teach the gifts or the anointing of the Spirit and never did I see any type of practice of the use of these gifts for the building up of the body. As a side note, I did learn much about church politics and doing everything according to policy.

I went to a conservative Bible college which took an even stricter stand against the gifts. I actually had to "lie" on my college application to be accepted into this university. I originally put that I took a position of "seek not, forbid not" as it applied to the gift of tongues, and the application was rejected. Since I had never seen a valid use of the gifts of tongues, I changed the application to say I'd never practiced it nor seen it utilized properly, and I would abstain from practicing it while attending the university. While at this conservative Bible college I was taught that the gifts ceased, because they were not needed any longer, that the complete cannon of scripture was all that was needed, and that those "sign gifts" were only needed to validate and give authority to the ministry of the early church.

There were differing viewpoints as to exactly when the gifts were no longer needed. One very respected author and pastor stated that after I Corinthians 13:8-13 the sign gifts are never mentioned again in the New Testament (yet they are). Others claim that once the last apostle died the gifts were no longer needed, still others claim that once the cannon was formed, then scripture was complete, and we had all that we needed to do what we needed to do. Some cessationists will take an extreme position that anyone practicing the gifts today are under the influence of Satan and demons, which reminds me of only one thing. It reminds me of when the Pharisees accused Jesus of operating under the power of the head of demons Beelzebub himself in Luke 11:14.

There is great controversy over I Corinthians 13:8-13:

> "Love never fails; but if there are gifts of prophecy, they will be done away; if there are tongues, they will cease; if there is knowledge, it will be done away. For we know in part and we prophesy in part; but when the perfect comes, the partial will be done away. When I was a child, I used to speak like a child, think like a child, reason like a child; when I became a man, I did away with childish things. For now we see in a mirror dimly, but then face to face; now I know in part, but then I will know fully just as I also have been fully known. But now faith, hope, love, abide these three; but the greatest of these is love."

The context of the chapter is that Apostle Paul was discussing love and how it never ceases and that everything in the world could pass away, up to and including spiritual gifts, yet love would remain. Yet it seems the main point of this passage is missed in favor of a pointless argument leading to much speculation, controversy, and ultimately division over spiritual gifts. What would appear from this passage is that at some point of full maturity, we will no longer need the spiritual gifts to encourage, edify, and comfort one another.

It is my humble opinion that there is no actual scriptural evidence that the gifts of the Spirit have been done away with. God has not left His children to accomplish the work He has commissioned us to do based solely on scripture. While I agree and whole-heartedly believe in the power, completeness, and total authority of the Holy Scriptures, I do not see any clear scriptural evidence that God removed the gifts from His children. I do believe that through neglect we have despised, confused, and abused the gifts of the Spirit and therefore quenched the Holy Spirit of God. However, that is our fault and we need to repent of it.

I also believe that there are passages that say the gifts will no longer be needed when we are mature and complete. I believe that time will happen when we cease to breathe air and are in the very presence of God Himself.

> "I thank my God always concerning you for the grace of God which was given you in Christ Jesus, that in everything you were enriched in Him, in all speech and all knowledge, even as the testimony concerning Christ was confirmed in you, so that you are not lacking in any gift, awaiting eagerly the revelation of our Lord Jesus Christ, who will also confirm you to the end, blameless in the day of our Lord Jesus Christ."
> 1 Corinthians 1:4-8

> "Beloved, now we are children of God, and it has not appeared as yet what we will be. We know that when He appears, we will be like Him, because we will see Him just as He is."
> 1 John 3:2.

The cessationist's position that the gifts have been done away with appears to fly in the face of scripture itself. Paul clearly tells us to pursue spiritual gifts. He goes so far as to say he wishes we all would seek spiritual gifts intently.

> *"Therefore, my brethren, desire earnestly to prophesy, and do not forbid to speak in tongues."* 1 Corinthians 14:39

> *"Do not quench the Spirit; do not despise prophetic utterances. But examine everything carefully; hold fast to that which is good; abstain from every form of evil."* 1 Thessalonians 5:19-22

> *"For just as we have many members in one body and all the members do not have the same function, so we, who are many, are one body in Christ, and individually members one of another. Since we have gifts that differ according to the grace given to us, each of us is to exercise them accordingly:"* Romans 12:4-6

> *"Pursue love, yet desire earnestly spiritual gifts, but especially that you may prophesy."* 1 Corinthians 14:1

> *"And God has appointed in the church, first apostles, second prophets, third teachers, then miracles, then gifts of healings, helps, administrations, various kinds of tongues. All are not apostles, are they? All are not prophets, are they? All are not teachers, are they? All are not workers of miracles, are they? All do not have gifts of healings, do they? All do not speak with tongues, do they? All do not interpret, do they? But earnestly desire the greater gifts."* 1 Corinthians 12:28-31

> *"For the gifts and the calling of God are irrevocable"* Romans 11:29

From reading these scriptures it is obvious that the Apostle Paul is instructing us to use something cessationism claims God took away. How terribly conflicting. In other words, go pursue something earnestly that God has or will soon take away from you. Have you heard the joke about telling the monkey to go in a round room and sit in the corner?

Again, it is my humble position that cessationism is a man-made idea and has no solid grounding in scripture. Many cessationists reference the early church fathers, Clement, Chrysostom, Origen, and Augustine (Ironically they fail to reference that even Augustine later in his life wrote the "*City of God*" and in chapter 22 reported extensively on a revival of miracles in his ministry). Referencing the early church fathers is good, but let us remember that while much of their writings were inspired by the Holy Spirit, they were still men, capable of making mistakes when operating in their flesh.

Many cessationists take scriptures out of context like the above mentioned 1 Corinthians 13 passage. Good hermeneutics and solid biblical study takes the whole of scripture and applies it in its entirety to address problematic themes and issues and is bathed in prayer and illumination by the Holy Spirit. To me, the cessationist position does not honor 2 Timothy 3:16-17, and since it proliferates the cessation of the gifts of the Spirit, it therefore calls question into the illumination of scripture by the Holy Spirit, the very Spirit they seem to almost deny except in creed or hymn. 2 Timothy 3:16-17 clearly states:

> "*All Scripture is inspired by God and profitable for teaching, for reproof, for correction, for training in righteousness; so that the man of God may be adequate, equipped for every good work.*" 2 Timothy 3:16-17

How crafty and sly the enemy is: cut out our life-giving source, cut out God on the earth with us today from the trinity, and let us attempt to do His work in our flesh. The result? Divorce, adultery, arguments within, rape, abortion, rejection, lies, human trafficking. It goes on and on. Satan's plan was great, and so many of us totally fell for it! Get them relying on their great ideas, have them teach a bunch of seminars on building the kingdom of God, get them busy doing good things instead of "God things". Encourage them to spend loads of time and money on completely worthless ideas to the point of being financially strapped and physically exhausted. Get them off track and focused on themselves, get them fighting over the gifts. Friends, I have to tell you, we have been duped. We have not been living and fulfilling our calling and destiny. I feel the need to say it again, the bride is dead, and the price tag is huge!

How did we think we could cut out parts of God's written word and customize it to fit our beliefs? There are whole passages of scripture that teach plainly the work of the Holy Spirit and the gifting yet we conveniently skip over them and claim to have a whole and sound theology.

I can honestly say in those early days of ministry I felt all along that I was really doing the work of God and building the Kingdom. If I am to be truthful, I was heaping on doctrines of my own making. I was repeating the things that "preached" well and sounded good. I can remember saying so many times to others that those who didn't share the same freedoms I did in Christ on lesser issues (music, dancing, you fill in the blanks) were Pharisaic and legalistic. Truth be told, they were, but so was I. I often said I wanted to be like the Apostle Paul. Perhaps like the Apostle Paul, I was "Chief Pharisee"?

I used to judge the nation of Israel and particularly the Pharisees, because they crucified Christ. I came to a point not so long ago where I began to ask these questions from a sincere heart. "How do you miss that Christ was the Son of God? How do you not only miss that, but you mistakenly thought he was a false prophet? How do you not only get there, but you go so far as to kill the Son of God?" I remember very distinctly going down the road one day listening to a podcast by a local pastor and pondering that very thought. I asked myself, "How did they miss it?" Then I heard the Holy Spirit speak to me almost audibly, "Mark, that's exactly what the church has done today. They murder me, because they have murdered the Holy Spirit."

I teared up and nearly threw up and just mumbled out the words, "You are right!" We have reproduced Good Friday and Easter. We have done the whole sad and sick story all over again; in our modern day and in our own high-tech way, we have murdered the Holy Spirit of God. We are modern-day Pharisees.

Folks, we are a dead bride, because we have chopped parts of God's Holy and inspired word out to fit a man-made theology. Remember the story I mentioned about the trip to Chicago and how we have treated God like our dog? The scenario doesn't just apply to those teens in that church. It is what most of us have done to God. We have made the Almighty into what we think He ought to be. The message that day didn't just apply to those kids in Chicago, it applies to you and me and the bride of Christ as a whole. We are treating God as if He were our dog. We need a much higher view of God than what we have right now, and the view needs to be accurate. We have adopted man's teachings, philosophies, and ideas on God, and we have forsaken His very word. It is strange to say it, but we will read a book (perhaps even like the one I am writing) about God, and we will not read and discern God's very words nor speak to God directly through the power of the Holy Spirit, even though this is our gift and source of illumination and power.

Please allow me to set something straight too in case there is confusion. If you are running to a particular gift (most likely the gift of tongues) as you read this chapter, I have to humbly ask you to get over it. I am not talking about the gifts in and of themselves. I think it is another downfall of the modern church. We seek the gifts and ignore the Giver of the gifts. We want His toys and trinkets and could care less about Him. We are like the crowds that followed Jesus because of His miracles. They followed Him because He could do magic or give them what they wanted, take away their pain, and make them feel better. How abusive, shallow, and fruitless. Just like those same crowds when Christ calls us to a cross, we run away leaving only the true disciples to do the work of Christ (John 6).

Have you ever stopped to realize that every miracle Jesus did was short-lived? The wine ran out again! The sick and lame eventually died, and even Lazarus himself died again. The gifts and miracles were not given for show or to just make people feel better. Christ Himself said He never did anything apart from the Father. The miracles He performed were performed under the careful guiding of God Himself. He wanted to make a point. Often the point was "I am God, and I can do anything! You can trust Me with your life. You can follow Me." He was trying to show us there is nothing that He cannot or would not do for those who sincerely seek Him. Most people today want to fight over specific gifts, especially the gift of tongues. I am not making a case for any particular or individual gift. I am sorry that some folks abused gifts. That doesn't mean we chop up scripture and create a man-made theology excluding the gifts. We find their proper God-honoring and body-empowering use and like Paul said, we *use them* as God intended for us to use them!

Well, there you have it. We found the murderer of the bride, and he is us!

If we stopped right here the story would be pretty bleak and hopeless, but please read on. One purpose of this book is to reveal the problem; however the greater purpose is to reveal hope. I believe there is hope for the bride of Christ. It is a primary reason I believe God has called me to write this book, to share hope with you. I believe our best days are yet to come! I believe we can make a difference, and I believe we will. I believe God is raising up a remnant in these last days, and He is about to do a work greater than He has ever done because of His great love and His great mercy for the world He died to save. The question remains, will you be a part of that great work?

CAN SHE BE SAVED?

Stop for a minute and let us take a look at how God works through His people. In Isaiah 55:8 God states that His ways are not our ways, and His thoughts are not our thoughts. Yet so many times we have tried to fight spiritual battles in fleshly manners and through our "great" human plans. We have tried to overcome the kingdom of darkness through our own human intellect, by human effort, and by our own discipline or power. Look throughout history and see how the church has handled its foes. We have tried open debate, boycotting, protesting, book burning, and even people burning. I am not saying we sit in a corner and let the world tell us how to live either. But didn't God Himself tell us in Zechariah 4:6 "Not by might nor by power, but by my Spirit says the Lord." Also in Ephesians 6:12 we are reminded that,

> "For our struggle is not against flesh and blood, but against the rulers, against the powers, against the world forces of this darkness, against the spiritual forces of wickedness in the heavenly places."

For some reason though we think we have evolved as a society and that the spiritual battles have all been won, and we can now move onto things handled through our iPad, social media accounts, and the latest proven-effective, slick business techniques. Where we run into problems is when we rely on our human intellect or wisdom to handle things that are of a spiritual nature. I fear most of my life I have done just that. I relied on my own God-given gifts to try to build God's kingdom as well as lead my family.

Did you see how close I came to being right on? "I relied on my own God-given gifts to build God's kingdom". That was pretty good, and I looked good trying. I heard the applause, and I got pats on the back. But I was so far off in most instances that I completely missed the mark. Did you know that some of the best lies are composed of 99% truth?

My own son, Joshua, had a few really rough years in high school when the enemy began to speak lies into his life, and he fell for it. The enemy got him as he usually does with some bait that seems innocent enough like music, drinking, or sex. Josh opened a portal, was curious at what the old devil had to offer, and invited him into his music. We as parents took a stand against what he was participating in as it was not his nature or destiny; we were against what it stood for and did not want him to hang out in that kingdom or with its inhabitants. The enemy very skillfully delivered the goods to Josh and told him we wanted to take away his fun and that he was really missing out. Same old junk as the Garden of Eden with Adam and Eve, just a different date and time and new characters. Well, long story short, Josh fell hard and found himself in a place of utter hopelessness, and he wanted to take his life on two separate occasions, because the enemy finally got him to a place where he believed there was no hope. God in His grace spared Josh's life and turned the story around to His glory just like He always does.

During this time, I too felt great hopelessness and frustration. I couldn't understand why Josh didn't just get it. All his efforts to run from God just got him deeper and deeper in trouble and caused greater pain to our family. I became embarrassed and in my flesh began to do things that only made the situation worse. At times I became violent, I screamed, slammed doors, called him names, and even got physical at one point. I hit Josh in the chest with a closed fist. It wasn't that the hit was so hard; it wasn't that I even hurt him physically. Worse than that, I hurt him deeply emotionally and spiritually. When I hit him he had a look in his eyes as if to say, "You are supposed to be my father. You are supposed to love me, not hurt me. You are supposed to pray for me, not reject me." I will never forget that night. I sent him to his room and sent myself to the couch and wept bitterly. I felt totally hopeless and felt like an absolute failure as a man, a father, and a Christian. I remember thinking as I wept, *I was a youth pastor. How could this happen to me and my family? What do I do now?* It was truly a dark, dark night in my soul and our home.

In desperation, I called an old friend in Omaha, Nebraska who God had radically transformed from a mean-spirited, selfish man into a man of great godly wisdom and grace. As I wept over the phone with him in hopelessness, sharing my story, he listened with compassion and even entered into my pain with me as he brought comfort from the other end of the line. Imagine my surprise when he began to laugh when I told him I hit my son. He told me, "Mark, you are trying to handle a spiritual issue in a fleshly manner. You could stomp that boy into a puddle and still not fix the problem." He began to share with me how my son had given ground to the enemy and was now a slave to sin. He needed a man of God, a godly father to step in and do battle for him, not against him. I began to realize I had made my own son my enemy instead of making Satan my enemy. He prayed with me that night. He prayed that the Holy Spirit would teach me, guide me, and give me great wisdom and discernment and most of all . . . *hope!*

I got up that night from that couch having learned a very valuable lesson. I knew all the verses about giving yourself as a slave to sin, but that night the Holy Spirit turned on a light switch and illuminated the subject. I saw that I had been fathering in my flesh, and it didn't do a thing except create a bigger mess. The very next night I talked to Josh as a different father, taking a different perspective. I told him what he had done was to invite Satan into his live and into our family, and Satan was playing for keeps. I explained that Satan hated him and wanted him dead. I explained that his only game plan for Josh was theft, death, and destruction. Yet on the other side, God loved him and had a great plan for him. I asked him if I could pray for his deliverance from this painful mess we found ourselves in. Josh was tired of the mess and agreed so I did what a man of God should do as a father. I laid hands on his head, and I rebuked the enemy from his life and took back control of my son to the glory of God. When Josh got up he sobbed uncontrollably and clutched onto me as if he knew one of us was about to die. He bawled on me for close to ten minutes, crying out for my forgiveness and repeatedly saying he was sorry for all he had done. That night God did something very profound and powerful through His Holy Spirit. For months and years I tried to handle things in my way, using my own ideas, but the battle was deeply a spiritual battle that had to be fought in the Spirit. In subsequent days we spent much time working through the mess he had created in his own life. For sure it has been a process, a long process, but one that has been possible because of the Holy Spirit's power in his life and mine. From that point on we saw it as a purely spiritual battle and fought it in our spirit and not in our flesh. The difference was night and day, oil and water, life and death!

I regret to say that my operation in my flesh spilled over into the rest of my family. I was harsh and unloving to my wonderful and loving wife. I did not lead and love her like Christ loves His wife (you and me, His bride). Instead of leading her, my words were unkind and spoke rejection into her life—a life that had already been littered with rejection for years. When she struggled spiritually and needed her husband to pray over her and tenderly walk with her into spiritual victory, I barked out orders and Bible verses and couldn't understand how she could be stuck in the same past struggles. I took a vow to love her and cherish her. I didn't honor that vow, instead I spoke rejection into her life. The man that she had dreamed about marrying, her spiritual leader, added to the rejection and pain instead of loving her as Christ loves His church. I look back at the wasted years and shake my head in disbelief.

The operation of my flesh was primary in my ministry and day to day living too. There were days of frustration, anxiety, and fear. I had to have a steady diet of Prozac and sleep aids for about six years while in the ministry. Again, I look back at the wasted years and the ones I could have really influenced for the Kingdom and I shake my head in disbelief.

However, I only shake my head for a few seconds. I have come to understand another passage of scripture, "Therefore there is now no condemnation for those who are in Christ Jesus." Romans 8:1. Today is a new day. I have come to understand that in our failures and weaknesses, He is strong.

Until recent days, I had never heard the message, "It's okay to fail!" How many of you have ever heard that message? I had a standard in my life of absolute perfection, and it was part of the reason I needed medication to cope with life. Do you know it is okay to fail? It is why God invented grace. He knew we couldn't live a standard of perfection, and He made a perfect plan to take care of our shortcomings, our bad days, weeks, and months and, yes, our failures. It is okay to fail as long as you make the most of your failure and learn from it, accept God's grace and move on.

When I fail, I can fail towards the cross, because my Heavenly Father comes along side of me and teaches me. He shows me His way if I call on His name. He is faithful too. He has shown me that my past is just that, it is my past. It is not who I am, and it doesn't own me. It doesn't dictate my future, and it isn't my identity. It is what I did. It is not who I am. I really hope you can get that because it is a matter of spiritual life and death. It is also a reason why I believe there is hope for the Bride of Christ. I believe there is hope, because it is His desire for her to be spotless and unstained, not dead or mortally wounded.

What can we do with her? What is the game plan to get back to where we need to be?

Remember back a few chapters I talked about "leaky gut"? I had the condition once. I was so frustrated because I had unwanted weight gain. I was always tired, couldn't sleep, and when I exercised it didn't seem to make a difference at all. I worked out in the gym as hard as I always had with limited results and probably more injuries than anything. I even went on multiple popular diets, working very hard at them only to see limited results. Finally one day a friend told me about applied kinesiology and a local doctor who practiced it. He jokingly referred to him as "the Witch Doctor" because of what he found in his life and health and how he went about finding it was very unusual and almost miraculous. As he shared his experience he was describing me to the "T". I went and saw this "atypical" doctor, and he told me I had leaky gut and gave me a series of herbs and minerals as well as a very specific diet to follow.

The following days and months were rough. I had to stay on a pretty strict diet and take handfuls of pills that tasted really nasty. One thing he gave me was a powder that had tree bark and moss in it among other tasty treats. When I first drank it I gagged! I nearly threw up the first several times I tried it. It wasn't what I wanted. It wasn't comfortable, and for the most part outside of a supportive wife who was doing it with me, I felt like a weirdo or freak . . . I felt alone. I felt sort of like a caveman eating my moss and berries and drinking my tree bark elixirs; however within a few weeks I saw the weight coming off. I started to sleep well and the muscle tone that I had lost was coming back. When I went back to the doctor after the initial treatment he explained that over the years I had polluted my body with junk food and had been depleting it of vital nutrition for so long that it was weak and sickly and needed repaired. When given the right ingredients, the body God gave me would actually heal itself and last a long time. Other than being tired and not able to get into the shape I desired, I had no idea I had the condition. I just thought I was "getting old".

I believe the same is true with the bride of Christ. I believe if she followed the simple formula presented in 2 Chronicles 7:14 God would uphold His end of the bargain. He said, "And My people who are called by My name humble themselves and pray and seek My face and turn from their wicked ways, then I will hear from heaven, will forgive their sin and will heal their land."

So often we hear people saying there is no formula to righteousness. God's grace is there so just ask for it. I want to push back on that for a second and say that there does appear to be a formula in this instance.

It is obvious this scripture was written to us. Sure you could make the point that this is an Old Testament passage, and it was originally intended for the nation of Israel, but then I will tell you to go back to the Apostle Paul's dissertation in Romans 11 where he says in His grace, God grafted us into His plan of redemption and thereby we became His people. Romans 11 is mind-blowing, because God extended such grace to us and has given us such an amazing opportunity. I think 2 Chronicles 7:14 gives us a formula that is timeless, and we need to at least give it a try. We aren't doing well otherwise, what could it hurt?

As you read this verse you might easily read over a very important word: "My". God is saying that this whole scenario begins with His people. As a nation, we could not be more deeply divided over the political issues of the day, and we are on the brink of disaster because of the division. We have heard and said for so long "united we stand and divided we fall". Well, a fall is in the making. God does not call us as His people to make the rest of the people repent. We, for some weird reason, think we are all Jonah telling the people of Nineva to repent as if we do not have any sin. We have done like Adam and Eve in the Garden and shifted the eyes of the Lord onto other's sins, acting as if we are not guilty. We have done the same thing as the garden, "God it is the woman you gave me . . ." "God it was the serpent . . ." We make excuses and blame others for the mess this country is in. We blame everyone for all the woes we face personally or corporately, and we do not look in the mirror.

We want to vote sin out of our country through the election process. We want to blame Hollywood and Washington for the problem. Read this verse again, it says "My people". It is written to us, not Washington, Hollywood, or your local strip club. It is time for us to look long and hard at both this verse and the mirror. The days of the church pointing its finger have to stop. We look and sound like Adam and Eve in the Garden of Eden, lined with cheap excuses trying to get the Almighty to look away while we serenade the devil. It is time for you and me to repent and address our own sins and let the others worry about theirs.

God says we need to humble ourselves. There could be a book on this point alone. I encourage you to put this book down and study the word humility in great detail. If you think you don't need to study it because you are so humble . . . stop, think about it . . . now go study!

I mentioned this in a rather crass manner when I said we castrated the trinity. Cross as it may sound, you have to ask yourself if it is true. We have insulted the Holy Spirit of God in a variety of manners, and we need to humble ourselves and just admit it.

The scriptures warn us about grieving the Holy Spirit or quenching the Holy Spirit of God (Ephesians 4:30 and 1 Thessalonians 5:19). Do we somehow think God is entertained or delighted that we in our arrogance have skipped over these scriptures and tried to handle things in our own flesh? Is there anything more arrogant than telling the Holy Spirit that He isn't there or, if He is, that He isn't needed, because we have it under control? We have done that by operating in our own strength and in the advice of others talking on behalf of God. We have been getting the whole person of the Holy Spirit wrong. He has been insulted, disrespected, misunderstood, and blamed for a bunch of stuff He never did wrong. He has been given a bad rap by people operating out of their flesh for their own gain. This is another lie the enemy has gotten away with for far too long. We have insulted the Almighty in the form of His Holy Spirit, and we are paying a terrible price, and we cannot afford, nor can the world afford for us, to continue on this path. Repentance and humility are in order.

Please understand something. As you read that last paragraph, the situation is now exposed and you need to do something about the truth revealed before your eyes. Please understand there *will* be a test on the material.

The next part of this verse says to pray. I am going to ask you again to put this book down. Right now you don't need to hear from me. I am just a man, a broken man with flaws by the truckloads. What you need to do is take some time in prayer. How long you ask? I have no idea. That is between you and God. I encourage you to get before the Almighty and ask *Him* to reveal to you the Holy Spirit just as He is. Ask Him to come and meet with you and to teach you what you need to know. Put away your theology books of the past, tell your dad and mom (that are yelling in your mind right now) to be quiet, and just speak directly to the Almighty. A spirit of religion will try to cry out against you, silence it in Jesus' name.

The enemy will try to stop your effort and for good reason. Right now it needs to be you and the Almighty alone, nothing more. You don't need a priest or some other person to do this for you. When Jesus died on the cross, the temple veil that separated humankind from the holy of holies was torn in half, from the top to the bottom. That means God welcomed you into His presence. Jesus did this for you. Utilize it and put it to work in your life in this critical moment. Enjoy it! Stop worrying that everyone will think you have gone nuts or off the deep end. Who cares what man thinks? You will not stand before a man one day in heaven. You will stand before your Heavenly Father. Ask the Holy Spirit to make intercession at the throne of God for you (Romans 8:26) and to reveal truth. Seriously, stop and put the book down. This is essential and reading further means nothing if you don't do this part. I'll wait, you pray.

I hope that the time you just spent was the best moment you have ever had in prayer. If not, try it again. If you skipped it, then the rest of this book probably is a waste of your time. Our repentance of what we have done against the Holy Spirit is absolutely essential. As you prayed, I hope it forever changed your life.

You see, God in this passage points out something very important, pray and seek my face. He doesn't say 'seek my hand', He says seek my face. What happened to Moses when he went on the top of Mount Sinai to meet with God? As he spent time in God's presence his face shined with the very glory of God. In this instance you and I are like the moon. The moon in and of itself doesn't have the ability to do anything by way of producing light. It has something in its DNA, its material makeup that simply reflects the light of the sun. Ironically enough, you and I are that way. We have something in our spiritual DNA that as we are in the presence of God, we reflect His glory, and we reflect His Son. The sick and dying world needs us to be in the presence of God, and then reflect His glory.

Know this too. As you are in the presence of God and experience Him (not another man or another created being) the very time spent in His presence will transform you; it will change you just like it changed Moses. Do you realize when you speak to God you are speaking to the same God that spoke to Moses? I cannot guarantee your face will physically glow, but I cannot say it won't either. Stay in God's presence, and let's see what happens. As He speaks to you through the Holy Spirit, as you worship Him, you will respond like Isaiah when he was in the presence of God. In Isaiah 6:5 we read, "Woe is me, for I am ruined! Because I am a man of unclean lips, and I live among a people of unclean lips; for my eyes have seen the King, the LORD of hosts."

You will walk away from seeing Him and realize your sinfulness and turn from it! You will hear from heaven, not hell, about your sinfulness, and you will repent of it and turn to God. When Satan speaks about your sinfulness, he speaks condemnation and judgment and that feels a lot like rejection, so you turn from God. This ultimately leads to your spiritual death. Many good people like you and I have been there and they turned away from God. Hear from heaven, reject the lies and condemnation. He forgives your sins, and He heals you! You will also better understand His immense love for you after these moments in His presence.

The important thing to remember is that revival and awakening begins with the individual. Please do not read this book and take the approach that your spouse, your kids, your neighbor, or your pastor needs to hear this. Please look at it from a very personal perspective and sing the words of the old song I heard in church as a child:

> "It's me, it's me oh Lord standing in the need of prayer.
> It's me, it's me oh Lord standing in the need of prayer.
> It's not my sister or my brother, it is me oh Lord standing in
> the need of prayer."

As each of us looks at how we have grieved and slandered the Holy Spirit, as He reveals to us our sin of eliminating Him from the trinity (His honored place as given by God the Father), and as we repent of grieving Him, He will show up. As He shows up in us individually, He will show up in us corporately, and the bride will breathe again. The blood will flow from her beating heart and course through her veins. The color will come to her face, heat will return to her body, and she will rise up to serve her husband if only for a short time. It will be a glorious time. It will be the time He envisioned when He left her and was away from her all that time. Can you imagine what it would be like if all of us walked individually in a spirit of revival? Can you imagine the synergy that would be created? It confirms what Christ said to Peter in Matthew 16:18 that the gates of hell would not prevail against the Bride! How could they?

A.W. Tozer, the great man of God, invested much time in His presence and heard from the Holy Spirit. He wrote a great many books about the Holy Spirit. He said the man or woman who truly lives in God's presence will bear three traits, or marks:

1. They will be lonely.
2. They will be misunderstood.
3. They will be uncomfortable.

Remember the diet I was on? I was lonely; nobody quite "got it" or understood me, and they were all too happy to watch me suffer. I can assure you as well that that period was very uncomfortable. I had dreams of chocolate milkshakes, Starbucks coffee combined with pizzas and cheeseburgers.

If you feel alone in God's presence, it's okay. The One who matters understands, and He's glad you are in His presence! You are healing your spirit. You are beginning a new, fresh adventure in your walk with God, and that's all that really matters. You are in the best place you could be, the presence of the Almighty. Stay there; it is where you were destined to be.

The verse continues to show us that as we humble ourselves, pray, and seek His face, He *will* hear from heaven and bring about healing. When we come to a point of realization that we have shot the Holy Spirit the finger, we can then realize how grieving and insulting this is to God. God calls us to confession and repentance not because He is wounded and demands an apology. We often see this in the human perspective when we are arguing with our spouse or a child, or perhaps when our kids are fighting. We often say we are sorry because it's seen as polite and usually gets the relationship going again. That is not what God needs. As we deal with our sin against the Holy Spirit, it is essential that we confess so *we realize* how disgusting and wrong we have been. When we realize the gravity of the situation and how grieving it is, we can then turn from it. When we realize who it is we have offended, the Holy Spirit of God, we realize His holiness and our sinfulness. It should be our deep conviction that we do not want to do that again.

We also realize where our arrogance has taken us, to the point of death as His loved Bride. Doing things our way has done nothing but create animosity, hatred, arrogance, and division. It has not furthered the cause of Christ. We have got to stop doing things our way. It doesn't work, and it is an absolute waste of time and resources, resources that are not ours in the first place.

But the beauty of the whole situation is God's grace. Even though we have offended Him and grieved the Holy Spirit, He will hear from heaven. He will, in His great grace, forgive our sin and heal our land. This is so like God! We offend, He forgives. We drive the nails, He forgives. We grieve the Holy Spirit, He forgives and heals! Do you see how crucial it is that we come to this point of repentance? We need to be here so we can be healed! This is the starting point; this is where our healing begins.

I encourage you once again, if you just kept on reading and didn't stop to spend time with Him, put this book down and spend time in the presence of the Almighty. We all are counting on you to. We need you to.

A PERIOD OF QUESTIONING
AND TRANSITION

For many years I tried to figure out what it meant to walk with Christ. As you can guess by reading about my many fleshly blunders, I tried to do this apart from the daily leading of the Holy Spirit and just could not figure it out. I was frustrated and knew there was more, but I couldn't put my finger on what it was. I had heard of this "abundant life" Jesus spoke of in John 10:10, but I wondered if I was even alive at all, let alone living in abundance.

I remember one time calling out to God in frustration, "Please God, help me. There has to be more than this." I was a pastor in a good church, but honestly, I was just playing a role. I was behaving and saying the right things (so I thought): keep God happy, keep your senior pastor happy, keep the elder board happy, and it will all work out in the end. While it flowed, paid the bills, fulfilled the routine, I knew something was missing.

God began to do something very profound and powerful in my life through multiple people and events. I think the first instance of the awakening in my life was when I was on the mission field in Reynosa, Mexico. I took a group of our young people and leaders there on a trip. One of my groups of kids were doing vacation Bible school and noted one little boy didn't come but his brother did. When they asked why his brother didn't come, the little boy said, "I'm wearing the pants". We found out that the poverty there was so bad these boys shared a pair of pants, so only one could go out in public at a time. Our kids were so moved by this that they found the little boy a pair of pants and took them to their house. While there, the mother came to the kids and said another of her children was going to die because of uncontrollable bleeding in his stomach. The doctors with their limited resources sent her home and said there was nothing they could do. I wish I could take credit for this, but I can't, as I was in a planning meeting for the next day's activity. These kids asked the mother if they could pray for the child. Of course she agreed if for no other reason than desperation. The kids laid hands on the child, prayed, and the child stopped crying and appeared to relax. They then returned to the base for the night. The next day not only did both of the brothers, wearing pants, show up, but the other child showed up too—not only alive, but completely symptom free. He even played soccer with the teens. I was absolutely blown away and speechless. But the kids acted like it was no big deal other than that it was really cool to be used by God this way. I began asking myself if I should be their leader or their student.

A year or so later, on another trip, a group who had prepared for street evangelism with a team of mimes was out doing their work when their youth pastor came upon a man sitting on a wooden palette. The palette had casters on it, and the man pushed himself along that way, because he couldn't walk. The youth pastor felt the Holy Spirit tell him to go pray for the man to walk! The youth pastor had a problem. He didn't "believe in that stuff." However, he somehow found the courage to approach the man and sheepishly asked him if he could walk. The man said that he hadn't walked ever in his life and was born that way. With butterflies in his stomach the size of pterodactyls, the youth pastor told him he was going to pray that God would heal him so he could walk. The youth pastor felt so afraid. He felt like a nut for even thinking this would happen. He gathered his kids around, and they all prayed for the man. They extended their hands to the man and helped him stand and walk for the first time in his life! They were blown away. Ironically, the staff that worked in the mission there was not surprised at all. They see this type of thing and much more on every mission trip they lead.

This really challenged my perfectly concocted theology and made me scratch my head in the spirit world and ask, "What in the world is going on here?" As I thought through these two episodes of miracles, I began to seek God and ask if there was a different God in Mexico or if I was missing something?

At the same time I had a friend who felt he was a missionary to his mainline denomination. He had had enough of the "common Christian life" (as he put it) and wanted an adventure. He packed up his family into a donated, old school bus and left for Georgia to join a mission's agency. He told me he wanted to live radical for God, and he was tired of trying to be in control. He began to talk to me and gave me that feeling of, "Oh boy, he's gone nuts."

This was about the same time the friend in Nebraska that I mentioned earlier had begun his transformation. His life had sort of blown up through circumstances, and he found Himself in front of the living God asking some pretty difficult questions. He too had grown up in church all his life but really didn't know the abundant life Christ spoke of. He hit the wall, the wheels came off, and God brought him to his knees in humility. He told me he found himself going to a church in the evening to hear a man speak about the anointing of the Holy Spirit. After listening to a sermon, he wanted to try what they were doing up front. He gathered up the courage to go up front only to have the special speaker tell him to return to his seat. He told him that gifts of the Holy Spirit are not a game or a toy and meant for the ones seriously seeking God. My friend left mad that night and vowed never to return to that church again, however he somehow found himself at that same church the following night. This time humbled and broken. He went forward again and asked to be prayed for.

He relayed to me the rest of the story in a nervous tone. He was cautious, because he knew I was against this type of hype and charismatic stuff.

He said he was "slain in the Spirit". I asked him in curiosity what it felt like. He said he couldn't really describe what happened. He just fell to the floor as if he were a dead man and was down for quite a while. When he came to, he felt a peace, joy, and love and began listing off the fruit of the Spirit. Mind you, these fruit were never a part of his life before. He went to the ground full of anger, anxiety, fear, and rejection but came up full of the fruit of the Spirit. It was as if he were a slow, old, junked-up computer, and God hit his reset button.

This caused me to question God even more. As I observed my friend's life over the course of the next several weeks and months, I realized something really did happen to him that night. Something had changed him. He spent hours each morning on his face in his living room, worshipping and seeking God. He spent time in God's word regularly. He began serving in the church, in ministries I never would have thought this guy would have served in. A guy who I once sought to minister to and help heal was now ministering to me in profound ways. It seemed that somehow he had blown past me in spiritual matters, though our pasts weren't much different. To see the transformation, to observe the changed lives around me, made me even more hungry to know what the truth was. I cried out to God even more to teach me, show me the truth.

The following summer I went to Iquitos, Peru as a guest speaker serving as mission trip pastor for a bunch of youth from around the United States. One day our teams were out doing door-to-door evangelism before lunch. We were out for a couple of hours and headed back to the bus, but we were missing one group of three: a big old boy named John and two younger girls. We waited and waited. They were holding up the rest of the group, and we were all getting pretty hungry. Finally, they slowly walked to the bus looking like they had seen a ghost. I began to scold them for making us all late and told them we didn't have time for goofing off and that we were hungry. Big John put his hand up to me as if to say, "Please wait and be quiet." All three of them could barely talk. After a few minutes John began to tell us they were having a bad morning. All the doors were being shut in their face, and nobody wanted to talk to them, which was very unusual as the people of Iquitos were pretty open to American visitors. They became very discouraged and began to head back to the bus early. Suddenly John felt as if the Holy Spirit told him to go to a specific hut and try there. Again, this is rough for John, because he didn't "believe in that stuff". He didn't know what to do or why, but he asked the girls and they both felt as if something was prompting them to go to the same hut.

When they knocked on the door, two elderly ladies came out to greet them. As they mentioned they were American missionaries and were telling people about Jesus, the little old ladies stopped them again saying they had their religion. Feeling somewhat foolish and rejected, John offered to pray for them and asked if they had any prayer requests. The first lady said she had "a terrible pain in her head as if a devil was living there". The other lady said she had "a terrible pain in her back that kept her from walking and sleeping some days". So John and the girls laid hands on their shoulders and began to pray the same generic prayer they had always prayed, "God help these ladies." Except when they touched the little old ladies something happened. John said he felt weak and like there was electricity flowing through him. He felt almost dizzy and thought maybe the heat was getting to him, but he continued to pray for the ladies to be healed. When they finished praying, both ladies were crying and asked if the teens could tell them more about their Jesus. The reason? As soon as they laid hands on them, the pains left their bodies, and it felt as if there was electricity flowing through them. They both received Christ that moment.

In the hut, John noticed there was a man sitting in a chair, and he was just rocking back and forth with a blank expression. John asked what his story was. The one lady said he was blind. John, filled with the Holy Spirit and not even knowing it, said, "Can we pray for him too." They said of course. When John looked into the man's eyes, he said it was as if they were filled with milk where his pupils were. They laid hands on him as well. When they finished . . . you guessed it, he was healed and had tears streaming down his cheeks. His eyes were as clear as they could be. He not only received his sight that day, he received Jesus as Lord and Savior and Healer. They all three were in church that night.

I was seeing things that didn't fit my theology, and it was making me very uncomfortable. I began to think maybe what I had been taught for years was wrong. Maybe there was something else I was missing. But I had been warned for years in the churches and bible colleges I attended that these things were done in the ancient church and were not practiced today. I was taught that the gifts of the Spirit were necessary to show a pagan and unbelieving world that Jesus and His ministry were legitimate and to plant seeds for the church. I was told that we had all the scripture we needed and that God didn't work like this anymore. I believed that anyone who practiced these things bordered on some kind of heresy and were scam artists taking money from people and building their own kingdom (and for the record, some were). I was fearful that all I had come to know as "truth" was about to be flushed down the toilet.

I began to wrestle with many fears at that time. I remember thinking, "What would my pastor of my home church think?" "What would professor so-and-so think?" "People will think I have gone off the deep end!" I asked myself, "How did this happen?" as if I had contracted a disease.

Isn't it a great tool of the enemy to stick these types of thoughts in our head to try to steer us away from the truth? How ingenious for him to stick some type of denominational name tag on the gifts of God to steer one away from the truth. Some at this point would argue that this is why we have denominations, to steer some away from heresy. It seems that is why and how denominations form. Someone attends a certain church denomination for a period of time until something is said or done that they disagree with, and then they go and form another denomination to fit their point of view as to what they believe the scripture teaches.

My question though is what is the truth as taught in the scriptures? Which denomination is 100% correct? There are some that argue they are the original church and have the pure truth, and the rest of us are perversions of the truth. These very denominations do not practice the use of spiritual gifts in daily walk and instead practice disciplines. There is nothing wrong with disciplines, creeds, and practices unless they keep you from the truth and the true spiritual power. I am not promoting nor condemning any denomination or group in this moment including the "Non"-denomination. I am simply trying to point out yet another tactic of the enemy, slap a denominational nametag on something to make it freakish and cause God's children to run from it in the name of heresy.

Friend, I beg you to get into God's word, get alone with God, seek His Holy Spirit, and tune out the denomination or your favorite teacher. Let God speak for Himself alone.

Over time, I found myself digging deeper and seeking more but struggling with what others would think of my newfound thoughts? I knew there were abuses of the gifts. I knew of countless frauds and phonies. Yet I knew what the denominations I grew up in taught. I knew what I was observing with my own eyes, and there wasn't anything phony about it. People were being healed, lives were being transformed, and Christ was being glorified. I was in a tough place for sure. I began to read some of the old great authors of the church. I bought books on the topic of the Holy Spirit. I began to dig deeper into the scriptures and open my heart to the teachings of the Holy Spirit.

As I began to share my teachings with friends and fellow church goers, I would often get "the look". You know the one that says, "What in the world is wrong with you?" Sometimes I even got the feeling people thought I'd lost my mind. I found myself talking with folks and no longer fitting in. I began to experience that scenario A.W. Tozer talked about: feeling a bit lonely, uncomfortable, and misunderstood.

I also began to feel uncomfortable in the church I was attending. I began to feel as if week after week I was being fed little to nothing. I began to hunger more and more for the things of Christ but wasn't getting much from the weekend service I attended. I thought I must need a small group, so I added that to my weekly activity. That didn't seem to work, so I added a men's Bible study, an accountability partner, and I did some serving. It seemed that all I really got was busy, but the nagging questions of the abundance Jesus spoke of and the power I observed was still not present in my life. I continued to call out to God asking Him to answer these questions.

I would say that this period of my life has been going on for over fifteen years. I know I am still in transition and learning more and more of His plan for my life every day. I continue to download podcasts of solid and accurate Bible teaching from a variety of teachers. I am plugged into a dynamic church with a staff that is gracious and loves the Bride. I am being refreshed. As I have reached out to God in the person of the Holy Spirit, He continues to teach me and grow me on a daily basis. I do attend Bible studies, and I do have an accountability partner, but the motive and the purposes are different. I am not working to find God's approval; I am working *from* His approval. The difference is everything, because the difference is life and death.

Through the period of questioning, I have found that God honors His word. He is a rewarder of those who seek Him (Hebrews 11:6). In my weakness, He is made strong (2 Corinthians 12:10). He is faithful. He will not allow us to be tempted beyond our ability, and He provides a way of escape (Hebrews 10:23, I John 1:9).

I have heard it said many times over, "How could a loving God allow bad things to happen to good people?" I think the question is the cry of the human heart. I also think it is a tool of the enemy to steer people from God. We need to stop asking, "Why?"

Allow me to illustrate how God taught me this principle. I have had things done to me that are considered bad by my standards, and as I whined to others, I found many who would agree that I was done wrong. I would often go to God and ask why He would allow something like this to happen to his prized and loved son. If I am saved, cherished, loved, forgiven, and walking in His favor, how could anything bad happen to me? (Mind you the scriptures are full of this type of thing happening to God's anointed, however somehow I missed them.)

One day I attended a Saturday morning Bible study, and one of our pastors spoke to us and shared what God had been doing in his life. He had lost a child earlier in his life and had found the strength and by God's grace moved on. Earlier that year, however, he had another unbelievable thing happen to him. He had a young daughter drown. They found her at the bottom of a swimming pool. Here is a guy who is serving God in children's ministry, and he was about to lose a second child to death. As he drove to the hospital, God told him it was going to be different this time. He was going to save his daughter and heal her fully. Weeks and months passed and while his daughter was alive, the prognosis was that she would never speak, walk, or live a normal life again, because her brain had been deprived of oxygen for too long. He sat months later, crying out to God, "Why? Why would you let this happen to me and my family?" In that moment, he shared with us that God spoke to him, and the words he shared would forever change my perspective. He said in that moment God asked him, "When are you going to stop asking 'why'?" As my friend sat there, he was left asking, "So, what's next?" It was as if God put him in a position where he had nothing left but to ask, "What's next?".

Has it ever occurred to you and I that God Himself through His Holy Spirit is about to unlock the heavens of blessings and miracles if we would just seek Him for the unbelievable? We get so stuck asking "why?" We lament our situation and stop having vision for what God can do. We get stuck, another tool of the enemy, and we lose sight of who God is and what He wants to do. When will we stop asking, "Why?" When will we start asking, "What's next?"

Others of us do the opposite. We know God's history and all the things He has done in the past and for others, but it doesn't seem to happen for us. We know that ultimately, in heaven, all things will be taken care of and yet we do not see Him in our current situation. We feel like Lazarus' sisters in John chapter 11. They called for Jesus to come and heal their dying brother Lazarus. Jesus showed no panic and no urgency to respond and waited two days before going to them. At this point Lazarus was good and dead. When Jesus showed up at their house, they are frustrated with Him, perhaps even downright mad. In verse 21 Martha says to Jesus, "If you would have come, my brother would not have died." She knew of the miracles Jesus did in His past. Jesus tells her that Lazarus will live again. Her response is in verse 24, "I know he will rise in the resurrection." She knew what Jesus could do in the future. What they didn't see was Jesus in their midst right there in front of them.

Another thing God has been teaching me in this time of struggle is that it is common for those He loves to go through a period of incubation to grow to where God has destined for them to be. Jesus waited for two days before He headed to Lazarus. Many of us think like Martha, if Jesus really loved them, He would have sprinted to their aid immediately. He revealed a clue to us in verse 15, "I am glad for your sakes that I was not there so you may believe."

Look at the example of Joseph in the book of Genesis. Early on in his life God gave him a dream. The dream was rejected by his family. The dream so bothered his brothers that they sold him into slavery, and they lied to their dad, saying he was killed by wild animals. (Talk about your dysfunctional family!) Though a slave, God was faithful to Joseph. His favor rested upon the young man, and he was promoted to the head of Potiphor's home. However, Joseph was put into the next period of transition and growth in the incubation process. He was a godly young man and apparently really handsome too, because Potiphor's wife was attracted to him, and she wanted him to give up his character and sleep with her. Poor girl, she wanted his character, but she only got his coat. Poor guy, he gets thrown into jail for doing the right thing. She lied, saying that Joseph came on to her, and he gets punished for years. You have to know in those dark, lonely nights Joseph was crying out to God wondering why bad things happen to good people.

Again, God was faithful, and Joseph was moved higher still to where he was over the entire land of Egypt during some of its most difficult times as it struggled through a famine. Shortly after taking the position of authority, who comes to town begging for food? That's right, his brothers, the very guys that sold him into slavery some forty years before. God molded this fine young man into an amazing leader and saved the lives of millions of people as a result. Why do bad things happen to good people? God has it as a part of His plan. God's thoughts are not our thoughts, and His ways are not our ways.

Notice though, Joseph goes through an incubation period of over forty years. How important was this? What was learned in the process? He learned the ways of an almighty God, and he realized that God was training and developing him all along through the good times AND through the difficult times. How do we know this? When his brothers arrived he didn't slaughter them! He was the most powerful man in all of Egypt. He could have had them tortured, humiliated, dragged before all of Egypt and had his revenge. His response though when his brothers feared this was "What you intended for evil, God intended for good." (Genesis 45:4-7) Through the process of the years of incubation, God provided a powerful man who understood His plan and was obedient to it with the skills, spiritual discernment, and guts to take a nation through some of their worst days. Have you ever wondered why it was forty years? Maybe Joseph's heart was so full of bitterness at what his brothers did to him. Maybe it was just God's timing. Who really knows? Does it really matter? God is God, and we are not!

What about the Joseph of the New Testament? His girlfriend/wife Mary tells him that she is pregnant. Joseph knows something is unusual here, because he has never slept with her. She is a virgin.

The story is so unusual and so difficult that God speaks to Joseph in a dream to assure him that this is part of His plan. Have you ever stopped to think of the faith of this Joseph to trust God in the midst of such bizarre circumstances? The lady that he loved tells him that she is pregnant. He knows he has not slept with her. He could have had her killed for committing adultery but instead the Savior of the World is born.

What was really at stake? Jesus' story could have been much different had Joseph not trusted God through a dream. Let me ask you how many other amazing stories do we cut short? How many times do we short circuit God's plan by acting out in our flesh, because we have not developed a relationship with God to clearly hear His voice and by faith take the next step to an amazing life.

Understand this, in the cases of our aforementioned Josephs, there was no history of God doing this type of thing. There were no Bible stories in Sunday school class of God allowing a young man to be sentenced to prison for upholding his standards. There were no stories of great men of God trusting that the Son of God was conceived in their girlfriend's virgin womb. They simply had to trust God at His word. We have to get to a point of trusting God. Instead of asking, "why", we must learn to ask Him, "God, what is the next step in your plan for me?" I think a great many miracles and opportunities await the Bride of Christ if we will take the next step in our incubation.

FINDING REST FOR OUR SOULS

Some of you as you read this book remember things from your past, and you know you have been hurt. The words of the last chapter may give you hope, however there is still more that you need. Some of you have been fighting the good fight, and you are tired, and you just feel as if you cannot go on any further. Let me assure you, I feel your pain. I want to take a brief second here to tell you about one of the most powerful and perhaps one of the most misunderstood gifts given to the bride of Christ, the gift of prophecy.

As I have been in my own spiritual incubator and as God has been developing my character, I have had some unbelievably dark days with intense spiritual warfare. I regret that I handled so many of these things in my flesh, yet God in His grace has used these opportunities to teach me how to handle them by His Spirit.

Our church provides an opportunity to come to the church to receive ministry from our prophetic ministers. As it stands right now, this ministry is so overwhelmed with requests they only have sign ups once a month, and space is limited. So many have seen the power of this ministry and its benefits that it has become so full that the number of persons gifted and properly trained cannot keep up with the demand. These ministers go through extensive training (about 9 months) on how to be led by the Holy Spirit, to accurately hear the prophetic voice of God, and how to properly minister these prophetic words to the body of Christ for edification, encouragement, and comfort. I have to admit, given my conservative background and upbringing, I thought the whole thing was pretty dubious until I went and experienced the gift in its proper context. I couldn't believe what happened to me that night as well as what happened to my wife and oldest son. To this day, I am blown away by how God is using the gift of prophecy in my life and the lives of those around me.

As I sat down in the sanctuary, there were two women serving in the group that I had never seen nor met in my life. I didn't tell them anything other than my name. They began by praying that the Spirit of Prophecy would speak to them and tell them the words I needed to hear in that moment. I sat with my head bowed and didn't have a clue what was about to happen.

The one lady spoke to me and said she saw a picture of me walking through a field struggling with some very tall, plant-like substances. She said I was pushing them back with my arms. When she asked the Holy Spirit what that was a symbol of, He told her I was trying to handle everything in my life in my flesh and that I needed to depend upon Him. This made my eyes open and my jaw drop. The words described exactly what I was attempting to do. But it was nothing compared to what was about to be spoken to me.

The next lady began to speak, and she had her eyes closed, her face grimaced as if in pain. She said, "Wow, you have been in some unbelievable spiritual warfare Mark. I see a battlefield, and the dead are strewn all over the place. Everywhere around you is death and destruction, and you are the only survivor. You are in a foxhole, scared, wounded, and tired." She explained in great detail the black clouds of the fires that burned on the battlefield. I felt as if she had been reading my emails or sitting at our dinner table each night. She then said, "I see you in the foxhole, your head is down. You are tired, discouraged, and deeply hurt."

What she then said was life changing. She said I needed to look up, for standing right above me was God, and He was reaching His hand down to lift me out of that dark and lonely place. He said He wanted to heal me and that the battle was over. I had fought valiantly and survived. I literally began pumping my fist in the air and tears came to my eyes. The battle in the previous three years was horrific, and I was so tired. Both ladies began to pray words of encouragement and blessings over me. They encouraged me to be in the word of God and in much prayer for His guidance. I can honestly say that night changed my life. Of course there were bad days, but nothing like what I had experienced in the past, and there was a new confidence and hope planted within me that God was taking me to a better place of rest and healing. Something happened that night, and I will forever be grateful to the prophetic team who ministers faithfully month after month, speaking words of encouragement into the lives of those that so badly need it.

As I met my wife and son that night, after they too received prophetic words from the team, I could tell they both had something similar spoken into their lives. They walked out looking as if they had seen a ghost. The neat part is that the prophetic words spoken in these meetings are recorded digitally and given to us to take home, study, write out by hand, and pray over. We seek God for confirmation, and if something doesn't line up, we know that the minister who delivered it made a mistake or heard something wrong and therefore we do not take the word spoken to heart. So there is accountability built into the ministry to reveal character and to keep to the truth. It also puts you into seeking mode to further understand what God is saying to you and to give you direction. My wife and son both shared their prophetic words with me and again with laser accuracy their words cut to their (and my) hearts.

I share that story with you for two reasons. First, the gift of prophecy is very powerful and extremely underutilized in the body today. Funny how for years we have debated the gift of tongues and Paul clearly tells us to not forbid it nor seek after it. He does, however, tell us to earnestly seek the gift of prophecy (1 Corinthians 14). But do we?

Again, I think Satan himself has twisted this gifting and its use to scare people away and perhaps cause confusion and ultimately dissension. Most people see the gift of prophecy as some almost mystical, fortunetelling game. We see the countless misguided efforts of the false prophets predicting the end of the world that are crafted carefully as if from the scriptures themselves. We see the misses (end of the world predictions are 100% misses to date), and we start to wonder if anybody can get it right or if every prophet is a false one. Again, leave it to Satan to twist a wonderful gift of God so we run from it. However, those words spoken into my life that night were from the heart of God, and I believe they changed the course of my life and ministry.

The second reason I share this story is that some of you are discouraged and have all but given up. Perhaps you *have* given up, and you badly need to hear a word from God Himself. You need edification, encouragement, and comfort. As I mentioned earlier, there is no shortage of bad news. It is all around us. Perhaps what you need is some good news.

I believe I have something for you. In the chapter on the enemy and how he works against the Bride, you related, didn't you? You have been hurt by a family member, maybe a spouse, a parent, or another in the body of Christ. You have grown bitter over the whole thing, and you honestly struggle with church, God's people, and you even find yourself hurting others as a result. You may even hurt those around you that you love. You don't mean to, but it just seems to happen.

When Christ died on the cross, He covered all of the power that sin has over you. The blood He shed for you not only took care of your sin itself, it took care of all of the effects of your sin and the sins committed against you. Jesus took the beating so you didn't have to. Jesus died so you didn't have to. God rejected Christ in that moment when all of the sin of mankind was heaped upon His back. God rejected the Son so you wouldn't have to face rejection. The price was paid. Isaiah 53:6 says "... By His stripes we are healed." When Christ died for you, He made it possible for you to be healed physically, spiritually, and emotionally. If you think any other way, you are short circuiting the work that Christ did on the cross. You are watering down and diluting the powerful blood of Christ and minimizing His work for you. It was all powerful, it was all encompassing, and you have everything you need for your life now and forever (2 Peter 1:1-11). What Christ did that day is absolutely astounding and incomprehensibly powerful. Once again, leave it to Satan to discredit what that moment in history did for us all. He hates that moment and will do all he can to wash it off the pages of history, because he realizes the power and freedom found in the cross of Christ.

In case you forgot, let me remind you that Satan hates God and consequently Satan hates you and me, because we are made in His image. God sacrificed His one and only Son, because He loves us so much. Satan does whatever he can to minimize or short-sell what happened at the cross, because it leads to freedom and life. He will do whatever he can to distract you from the cross, from going there yourself, and from leading others to that cross, because Satan had his lunch handed to him for all eternity in that moment. The cross and subsequent resurrection of Christ spelled his defeat ... period!

Why am I saying this? Because Satan takes whatever he can in your life, past, present, or future, and he seeks to sideline you with it. If you watch any sporting event today, one of the biggest questions before games is "who is hurt?" The opponent is hoping that your star player is on the bench with injury or illness. Satan plays the same way. He wants you on the bench. He will do whatever he can to put you there through injury or illness. You see, your soul is not up for grabs. It is sad that many in the church today are in the grasp of a false belief that their behavior is the final glue that holds together their relationship with Christ. They falsely believe they are able to operate good enough in their flesh to keep God happy enough to allow the work of Jesus to be enough in their lives. Their formula for life is the work of Christ on the cross, plus their adequate behavior, means they are allowed to enter heaven. This dance can be very tiring, and unfortunately many live a lifetime dancing to that song, hoping to get a hug from God. After years of dancing and ultimately fatigue, many give up and miss all that Christ has for them. This is yet another trick of the enemy.

Still others have been hurt, have grown bitter, and refuse to play the game. In multiple strange ways, they take themselves out of the game. They are wounded and sit angrily on the sideline criticizing everyone and everything that the church does that doesn't meet their standards. They sit there and complain about the pastor's sermons, their families, and how they could do it much better. I have a friend who once said if we could get these types to study the word of God as carefully as they study the every move of the pastor and his family, we'd have one amazing body! Instead of being in the game and serving, they criticize the ones who are. Their standards for others are too high and often for themselves the standards are too low.

Still there are others who have been wounded, and they just give up completely and never walk into the life that Christ has provided for them. They are afraid of the pain that came with the injury, and they don't want to experience it again, so they sit quietly on the sideline. It is easier to sit than go through the pain.

I recently heard a pastor speak of the abundant life. As I sat in the front row with my wife, he asked if anyone had a coupon in their possession. My wife, being the coupon queen, had more than enough to share. As he took the coupon, he shared that when Jesus said He came so we might have abundant life, He was simply giving us a coupon. A coupon gives you the right to whatever it is the vendor is offering you—perhaps a free sandwich, drink, or an amount off of their product or service. You cannot eat or drink the coupon, and if you read the fine print, it has no cash value. It does however give you the right, or opportunity, to cash in on its benefits. When Christ said I came to give you abundant life, He provided you with a coupon of sorts. It is up to you to cash it in by walking into all He has provided for you. Satan understands this concept better than most Christians and lies, deceives, and does whatever he can to keep you from walking into that Promised Land. He just has you hold onto the coupon, hoping that you will run it past its expiration date and never use it.

We sit and judge the people of Israel walking around the desert for forty years when the Promised Land was only an eleven day walk from Egypt. Yet some of us do the same thing, wandering around a spiritual wilderness for a lifetime complaining about our leaders and never walking into the land God has promised us.

When someone hurts you, Satan and his thugs are right there waiting and they get into your thoughts to blow things way out of proportion. He piles lies on lies, tells you things to destroy your hope, and inserts fear in places where God has intended joy and boldness. He works against us continually and has been successful at doing this for years. He realizes he cannot have your soul. Christ paid the price, you are His, and the issue is not up for negotiation. The contract between you and God for your soul will never go up for renewal, and God does not sell off mortgages because He has found some that are better than others. He is not going to let go of you, and Satan is not powerful enough to take you away from Him. In John 10:28-30 He says,

> *"And I give eternal life to them, and they will never perish; and no one will snatch them out of My hand. My Father, who has given them to Me, is greater than all; and no one is able to snatch them out of the Father's hand. I and the Father are one."*

Knowing that you are not up for grabs, Satan does the next best thing, he works to neutralize you. He does whatever it takes to render you ineffective. If he cannot keep you from the kingdom, he will keep you from your gifts. He robs you of joy with worry, doubt, and fear. He attempts to strip you of your identity as a cherished child of the Most High. He takes away your fellowship with other believers in the body with bitterness and lies that people of the church do not like you, and you do not fit in. He tells you that your spiritual gifts are small and insignificant, and nobody really cares about them. He tells you that all of the promises of the Bible are for others and that somehow you are an unusual case and so don't even bother trying. If you do try, he will magnify any small issue to inflame discouragement so that you do not try again.

Whatever he can do to steal your joy in Christ and sideline you is good enough. He knows the power of synergy that can be created when all God's children are walking in grace, power, and the gifts of the Holy Spirit. So he works hard to neutralize us. He realizes if we all got together in unity, if we all walked led by the Sprit, that the synergy would blow the gates of hell wide open, and there is absolutely nothing he can do about it. That's why he has worked so hard to injure the body of Christ. I dare say, he has had significant success.

He is in fact a roaring lion. It says so in the scriptures. But he has been caged since the death and resurrection of Christ, so all he can do is roar and swipe his paws against the bars of that cage to intimidate you and I. Know this though; you have authority over him and his works. No weapon formed against you shall prosper because of the great work of Christ. You have the coupon; you just need to use it! Redeem it. Christ paid the price. To not use the coupon is a total waste of His sacrifice and your potential and destiny.

One of the purposes of this book is to give a shout out to all those that are hurt. It is the one group I feel God is calling me and my family to minister to. It is hard to believe how many of us are hurting in the body. We sit in the pews and seats of the church week after week silently suffering, afraid to share for fear of what others might think of us. Satan laughs. It has been effective. Until now!

If you have been hurt, I am certain your hurt is real. I don't doubt that, and I wouldn't dare downplay your pain. But your injury keeps you from serving and blessing the body of Christ. The price has been paid.

In reality, there is no reason for you to continue in that hurting place. There is healing for you. Christ paid the price and has a small army around you. You have to reach out and get healing for your wound so you can get back in the game! We need you! We need your gifting, and you show the power of Christ and the Holy Spirit in your healing.

Did you know that every time Satan hurts you he gives you the opportunity to have a testimony of the grace and goodness of God? That's right! Every time he wounds you he runs the risk of advancing your cause for Christ. It is almost crazy how risky it is for him to come after you. Don't believe me? Go back to Joseph of the Old Testament. Every time he was wounded, his wound was deeper and deeper. Every time he suffered a setback in his life, he went further down into deeper pain. Yet every time he rose to new heights until he was one of the most powerful and prominent men in the land. If only we would trust God instead of embracing our wound. For some of us, we are so familiar with and comfortable with our wound that it is like a family pet.

It is time to release the pain and wound to Him for His healing. He is faithful, and He will heal you and take you to new heights, and your story will bless those all around you. Look, the book of heroes isn't closed yet. There may be one more chapter to be written, and it might be your story. If you have been hurt, ask God to lead you to the source of healing. He alone is our Healer, and He will use others who have gone before you in hurt and brokenness to bring about your healing. Come on, get back in the game. We need you!

A DEMONSTRATION OF POWER

So where do we go from here? I have always believed a good minister of the gospel is one who doesn't necessarily give all the answers. Rather the best are the ones who create within us a hunger for the Holy and cause us to seek God with more questions. I have attempted in this small work to do what I believe God has called me to do. To awaken a bride that has fallen asleep.

Maybe you don't agree with all of the points of this book. Maybe you feel like my case is weak. Maybe you think things aren't so bad, and I am stuck in a small corner of the world not getting the big picture. Maybe you are right and, well, maybe not. I think it is safe to say at the very least, we can do better . . . much better.

My intention of writing this book is to stir something up in the bride of Christ, to create a searching process. I sincerely want to bring about a resuscitation of sorts to get her breathing again, and I confidently believe she will see her best days. We serve a God of miracles, and He always allowed His people to come to the end of the rope, to hit rock bottom, and then He steps in and works a miracle so great that only He can take credit for it. I believe our best days are yet to come.

I am seeing within the body of Christ an awakening of the spiritual gifts in healthy manners. I am not talking about the extremes and abuses; I am talking about the gifts being used in the manner God intended them for.

In Acts chapter 2:16-19 it says:

> ". . . but this is what was spoken of through the prophet Joel: 'AND IT SHALL BE IN THE LAST DAYS,' God says, 'THAT I WILL POUR FORTH OF MY SPIRIT ON ALL MANKIND; AND YOUR SONS AND YOUR DAUGHTERS SHALL PROPHESY, AND YOUR YOUNG MEN SHALL SEE VISIONS, AND YOUR OLD MEN SHALL DREAM DREAMS; EVEN ON MY BONDSLAVES, BOTH MEN AND WOMEN, I WILL IN THOSE DAYS POUR FORTH OF MY SPIRIT And they shall prophesy. 'AND I WILL GRANT WONDERS IN THE SKY ABOVE AND SIGNS ON THE EARTH BELOW . . .'"

That reference was used on the Day of Pentecost when the early church first began experiencing signs and wonders to show the world that God is the Almighty. God was, if you will, flexing His muscles to leave no doubt that these apostles were of His kingdom, and He was all powerful. The Apostle Peter stood up filled with the Holy Spirit and announced that these signs and wonders were showing the hand of God as promised from the prophet Joel in Joel 2:28.

I believe God is performing CPR on His bride, and I believe He is getting ready to come get her and take her home. I am not predicting dates. I want to talk very practical right now and share my heart. I believe God in His grace is pulling things together and wooing us to repentance and reconciliation, for the time is short.

I came to realize the first time I took a spiritual gifts assessment that I rated high in the gift of prophecy. Truth be told, I had no clue what the gift really was or how to use it. It has been in recent days I have received solid Biblical teaching on how to serve in this wonderful gifting. Usually it is common for those who have the gift of prophecy to also have powerful visions and dreams. I have had these at multiple times in my life, however I never knew how to utilize the gifts and serve the body of Christ. Ignorance of spiritual gifting is no excuse. It is vitally important to both you and the body of Christ that you seek out a good spiritual gifts assessment and learn how to serve using your gifts the way that God intended for you to.

A couple of years ago I had a dream, and when I awoke, there was no doubt as to why I had it and what God wanted me to take away from the dream.

I had a dream in which my family and I were in our cabin aboard a luxury cruise ship. We were fooling around in the cabin, wrestling and laughing, when there was a gentle knock at the door. I went to the door and opened it and was greeted by a distinguished, clean-cut, handsome older gentleman dressed in a black sailor's suit. It was the Captain of the ship! He calmly greeted me and said, "Good evening. I am so sorry to bother you, however I need to inform you that the ship is damaged and sinking, and I need all of you to get your life vests and make your way to the lifeboats. Please be calm but be purposeful. Do not bring anything except the clothes you have on. Thank you."

He calmly stepped away from the door and made His way down the hallway. I turned and closed the door and like any typical human being, I yelled to my family in panic and told them in fear, "Hurry up, get your life vest, the ship is sinking!" Immediately they too panicked and began grabbing all sorts of things. My wife grabbed our family photos and keepsakes. My sons grabbed video games and other things that young boys would. I shouted again in panic, "Forget that stuff, we don't have time! Just get your life vest and let's get to the lifeboats." We opened the door and began to head out.

I looked down the hall to the right and saw the Captain telling another group in their cabin the same thing in the same calm, gentle manner. What was strange to me though was he was not going to every room, only certain ones. It seemed odd to me, but I didn't dwell on it, because we had to get to the lifeboats. As we walked through the ship in a rapid fashion, it was as if nothing was happening. I passed by a lady wearing an expensive and beautiful white dinner gown sipping a glass of red wine. She was certainly in no hurry and showed no signs of panic. I asked her, "Ma'am, don't you know the ship is sinking?" She replied, "Yes, I know, but we have a lot of time. It will be okay." I shouted back to her, "No ma'am, the Captain told me we need to get to the lifeboats, you need to hurry. The ship is sinking!" She paid me no mind and turned away, sipping her glass of wine. We began once again hurrying to the life boat. It seemed as if nobody else cared, and no one was wearing their life vests nor making their way to safety. I passed by the casino, and it was full of fun-loving people who were gambling away at poker tables and slot machines as if nothing was wrong. I couldn't believe nobody was going to the lifeboats.

At that moment I woke up and realized it was just a dream. My heart was racing, and I was sweating. I laid back and put my head on my pillow and looked at the ceiling. *That wasn't an ordinary dream though,* I thought to myself. I began to pray, "God, what was that all about?" Never before have I had such clarity in hearing the voice of God as I did in that moment. God spoke to me and said, "Mark, the end is coming near. You need to gather the ones that you love that I have entrusted to you and get your house in order. The ship is sinking." I replayed the dream over in my mind as I laid there and thought about each aspect of the dream. I believe the Holy Spirit gave me understanding of what things meant.

In our cabin, we were playing and living life as normal; having no idea the ship was damaged and sinking. The Captain, God, came in a calm manner to warn us gently to go to safety and leave behind the things that really don't matter. He goes door to door but only to those who "have ears to hear" and will give heed to His words. The lady in the white dress sipping wine and those in the casino are the majority of people. They have heard the ship is sinking, but they feel as if there is plenty of time and there are better things to do. The majority of people really does not care and are busy with the things of life.

I really felt as if this dream was a wakeup call to me to get my house in order. I want to share it with you to make a simple point. I have seen and heard about many people having the same experience as I did. There seems to be a great awakening of prophetic gifts manifesting in dreams, visions, and other prophetic words like never before in the church. It is as if we are seeing a Pentecost again. Could it be that God ushered in the church age with such giftings and manifestations and He is now beginning to usher out the church in the same manner? I believe we must be on the lookout. As God increases the dreams, visions, and prophetic voices, Satan too will step up his attack of false dreams and visions, and false prophets will abound. We must be more discerning than ever.

One day I was reading the scriptures and came across this passage in I Corinthians 2:1-5.

> "And when I came to you, brethren, I did not come with superiority of speech or of wisdom, proclaiming to you the testimony of God. For I determined to know nothing among you except Jesus Christ, and Him crucified. I was with you in weakness and in fear and in much trembling, and my message and my preaching were not in persuasive words of wisdom, but in demonstration of the Spirit and of power, so that your faith would not rest on the wisdom of men, but on the power of God."

The Holy Spirit spoke to me and showed me that the Apostle Paul didn't come to the bride of Christ with slick illustrations, humorous stories, and PowerPoint presentations. He came in humility, in his weakness, and most importantly in demonstration of the power of the Holy Spirit. I never heard anyone teach me this in Bible College or any of those expensive seminars or conferences I went to. I did, however, hear much about slick stories, perfect outlines, and having your game face on.

I think what has happened to the body of Christ is that we have relied upon our man-made ideas and philosophies, denominational name tags, heritage, and our own intellect rather than an anointing of the Holy Spirit of power. We suffer to the point of death and irrelevance today as a result. I think the whole cessation teaching is man-made. It leads to works of the flesh, and it has led our own version of spiritual leaky gut. I think time is short and I think we, as a collective body of Christ, need to stop relying on our flesh and our college degrees and step away from man-made ideas and return to the power the Apostle Paul speaks of, out of our own weakness, trembling, humility, and fear. I think it is time we seek out the real source of power that will populate the kingdom of heaven and set people truly free from addiction and bondage and empower them to do the work of ministry.

I also think some of us would be surprised if we knew the story behind so many great and powerful saints of just a few decades ago. I was absolutely intrigued with the founder of Moody Memorial Church and Moody Bible Institute Dwight L. Moody and the powerful evangelistic ministry he had. He was legendary and considered by many as the most effective evangelist of the nineteenth century. It is said of him that "he shook two continents for Christ." His ministry continues to live today, long after he went on to be with his Savior in 1899. The man was absolutely unbelievable and said of himself:

> "Someday you will read in the papers that D.L. Moody, of East Northfield, is dead. Don't you believe a word of it! At that moment I shall be more alive than I am now. I shall have gone up higher, that is all; out of this old clay tenement into a house that is immortal—a body that death cannot touch; that sin cannot taint; a body fashioned unto His glorious body.
> I was born of the flesh in 1837. I was born of the Spirit in 1856. That which is born of the flesh may die. That which is born of the Spirit will live forever."[1]

As a boy I heard of the great evangelist Moody, who was once a common shoe salesman. One thing I never heard about D. L. Moody was how he pulled it off. What was his game plan? What was his source of power? What was it that made him such a great evangelist? It wouldn't appear that it was anything in his flesh. On his first attempt to obtain membership in the Church of Mount Vernon, he was denied. His first Sunday School teacher, Mr. Edward Kimball, said he hadn't seen such a spiritually darkened mind and didn't think there was anyone less likely to fill any legitimate public gospel ministry.

Where did he get the charm or training to be so effective in ministry? Moody himself explains the secret (not to be confused with "The Secret" running around in modern days) in a little known book he first wrote in 1881 entitled "Secret Power". In this book, he shares how his life and ministry were transformed while visiting New York City when he cried out to God and asked for more of His Holy Spirit. He said he could not describe it and didn't talk much of it because the moment was so sacred. He claimed his sermons weren't different, and there were not new truths presented, however hundreds were converted. Many would stand back and say he was a hardworking, deep theologian who had some kind of "God luck" yet Mr. Moody himself would say of the Holy Spirit:

> "How much we have dishonored Him in the past! How ignorant of His grace, love and presence we have been. True, we have heard of Him and read of Him, but we have had little intelligent knowledge of His attributes, His offices and His relations to us. I fear He has not been to many professed Christian and actual existence, nor is He known to them as a personality of the Godhead."[2]

To quote my teenage son, "Boom!"

I would challenge you to search long and hard and find a copy of his book and discover what it was that caused a common shoes salesman to shake two continents for Christ and see if there is something you can find in there to help you change the world in which you live and bring about that demonstration of power the Apostle Paul referred to. I believe our time is short. I believe that never before in history has a lost and dying world, that God so loves, needed the church to be the bride that she is called to be. I think that today we need now, more than ever, demonstrations of the power of God in place of our slick or humorous stories and man-made, cute outreach events. We need something to come from our churches that has eternal significance and the power to transform lives by the thousands, like the church had in Acts 2.

I believe that in these days, like the Apostle Peter spoke of the prophet Joel, God is beginning to pour His Spirit out upon mankind, and we are just beginning to see evidence of this work. My question is: who will join in? I believe that God led me to step out in faith and write this little book, somewhat like he did the evangelist D. L. Moody, to share the truth that the church has been neglecting His source of power, the Holy Spirit. I believe God is acting in grace toward His dead and irrelevant bride, trying in love to bring her back to life to reach the world in perhaps the greatest revival in church history. Will you join in?

I see throughout the country, and hear stories of churches around the world, that people are stirring in the power of the Holy Spirit and care not about the lifeless doctrines of man any longer. I hear of the common businessman in Ohio who is tired of the week in and out routine and is finding out about the power of the Holy Spirit. I hear about the youth pastor in Philadelphia in the mainline church who has teens asking him what's missing, and he, like me, is going on an adventure to find out about Moody's "secret power". I hear of the young wife and mom who grew up going to church on the church bus who is tired of not having the abundant life Jesus promised in her day to day walk. I am telling you, God is stirring up the bride. Are the angels wetting their lips to blow the trumpets and usher in the Savior's return? None of us know for sure. However Jesus gave signs of His return, and I think we all see strong evidence that many of those things are in place and may have been in place for years. Are you ready?

Are you tired of the daily routine where you find yourself going to work, coming home, struggling to sleep, and doing it all over again tomorrow? Week after long, busy week passes by. Do you find yourself asking, "Isn't there more to life than this?" Are you tired of going to worship services week after week and hearing good messages but not experiencing any real power to give you victory over sin and power in reaching the lost and power to sustain you through the week?

Moody said it so well:

> "If we work . . . to some definite purpose, we must have this power from on high. Without this power, our work will be drudgery. With it, it becomes a joyful task, a refreshing service."[3]

Are you looking for it too?

Notes:

[1] Paul Dwight Moody, Arthur Percy Fitt, *The Shorter Life of D. L. Moody, Volume 1*. The Bible Institute Colportage Association—1900, P9.

[2] Dwight Lyman Moody, *Secret Power*. Fleming H. Revell Company, 1881, P23.

[3] Dwight Lyman Moody, *Secret Power*. Fleming H. Revell Company, 1881, Preface.

STAYING IN THE FLOW

I pray as you have read through my humble book, you have stopped to ask a lot of questions along the way. It is my prayer that this book and the journey have been transformational for you. If you still have questions, which I admit I do too, I pray that you will seek the Holy Spirit. This I know: we have the promise throughout scripture that as we seek Him, He will be found by us.

No matter what you have heard about God, know this to be true. He loves being found. He loves the chase for sure; however He really loves being found. He wrote the story of the prodigal son. He is that father who looks out the window everyday waiting for you to come home. He is that father who runs as soon as He sees you on the horizon, and He runs out to you! He doesn't care that you smell like pig and all the stuff pigs smell like, you are His . . . and He loves you. You haven't been living your heritage; you haven't been at His table where you belong. He is that one who will leave the ninety-nine sheep to come find *you*, that one little single lost sheep. He's already proven it for you. He is that one who went to the cross of Calvary and faced the physical horror and torture mingled with utter humiliation so that He could bless you with His presence for all of your life and for all of eternity.

Know this, whoever has sought earnestly after God has ALWAYS found Him. He has said He rewards those who seek Him (Hebrews

11:6). What a reward! Can you believe it? Finding Him to have relationship with *the* Almighty God, *the* King of all kings and Lord of lords? I trust that in the pages of this book you have found Him. But if you haven't, keep seeking! I promise He will be found. More importantly He promised it, and He's never lied.

Maybe you are one of the ones who read this book that have been wounded and sidelined. Please know you share a special place in God's heart too. I know firsthand, I have been there myself. I hope you have found healing for whatever it is that has been keeping you out of the game. Know this too, Satan doesn't care what it is as long as it keeps you from using your God-given gifts and serving both King and kingdom. Satan doesn't care how you fall out of the boat. You can fall out of the left side or right side, through conservatism or liberalism, just fall out and stay in the icy waters. That's all that matters. So I pray that you have at least begun your road to full healing and recovery.

So perhaps you have found Him, what next?

One of our pastors shared an illustration that was so profound it etched itself on my forgetful mind. He was teaching on walking led by the Spirit as a lifestyle. He spoke of how so many times we visit church and get a filling, only to have it empty out within the week. He said sometimes we hit a conference and get really charged up to overfilling, however over a span of time it runs out. Some of us think we need to get a bigger cup to hold a bigger blessing and filling. So we get a bigger cup by studying the Word more and attending more seminars and services and add a few Bible studies with other friends or co-workers. Sadly though, once again, we still find ourselves emptied, dry, and in need of filling. So we think maybe we need a better or maybe more ornate cup! So we upgrade the cup to something shiny and metallic and maybe even bedazzled so it is pretty impressive to others (and that way nobody can see what's on the inside). Yet that doesn't fix the issue. Those types of cups run empty too.

Maybe you find yourself here today. You have tried many different cups. You have tried the different shapes, sizes, and colors but find yourself out in the world and feeling empty.

What our pastor did that day was a great illustration to show how we remain full of the Holy Spirit as a way of life. He had a tall, white pedestal with a large (five gallon) water dispenser full of blue water sitting on top. The beautiful white pedestal sat in a reservoir, and there was a small tap at the bottom of the pitcher to dispense the blue water. He sat the smaller clear cup under the spout and simply turned on the water. He left the water on, and it filled the small cup and overflowed, running down the pedestal and into the reservoir. He just left the cup there and let the water run all over the pedestal and into the reservoir.

This is a beautiful picture of what God has designed for you and me to stay in the flow of His power and grace. Of course even the 5 gallon container would run out eventually. But His power knows no end. He is not limited or else He would not be God. It is our job to just stay in the flow.

In John 15:5 Jesus said it very simply. Sometimes things so simple get missed completely. He said, "I am the vine, you are the branches; he who abides in Me and I in him, he bears much fruit, for apart from Me you can do nothing."

How can we possibly live the Christian life apart from the life of Christ? We can't. Simply stated, we must remain. We must remain in the flow of the power of His Spirit. What we must seek to do is abide, remain, and stay in connection with His Spirit. We make things far more complicated than they need to be. We try to decorate the cup, hoping it will somehow make things better. We try to make the cup bigger with more works and activities but only complicate things. He simply wants us to remain.

I thought maybe it was tougher than that. There must be some hidden meaning in the Greek or something. So I looked it up. I mean come on, there has to be more to it than that. Here's what I found. The word abide in the Greek is *Meno*, which means to abide, wait for, be, be present, continue, dwell, endure, remain, stand, or tarry. That doesn't seem that hard, does it? In fact, it seems pretty simple. Why is it that we make things so difficult? I can only imagine the grapes on the grapevine struggling to stay on the vine. He has called us to seek Him; He will be found, and then we just remain.

Maybe I have oversimplified it a bit, I will admit. We have a real enemy, and we live in a fallen world. I know firsthand that remaining is a lot harder than it sounds. I think it comes down to focus.

Again the Apostle Paul wrote, in Philippians 3:13-15,

> *"Brethren, I do not regard myself as having laid hold of it yet; but one thing I do: forgetting what lies behind and reaching forward to what lies ahead, I press on toward the goal for the prize of the upward call of God in Christ Jesus. Let us therefore, as many as are perfect, have this attitude; and if in anything you have a different attitude, God will reveal that also to."*

Can I ask a favor of you my friend? Can I go so far as to beg you? Would you please put your past behind you and run for the prize? What happened in the past in you, around you, or to you doesn't really matter. The past is just that, it is the past. You cannot go back and undo it, you can only leave it there. Our enemy Satan will try to chain you to your past. He will tell you it is who you are, that it is there forever, and you will never outrun it. Remember he is nothing but a liar. Step into the truth on the matter: if you have given your past to Jesus, it is done. Our pastor says it so well, the grace of Jesus doesn't alter your past, it alters your future. Isn't that great news?

Starting today, begin a habit of crying out to God like D.L. Moody and ask Him to show you the fullness of the Holy Spirit and teach you what remaining looks like. Then as you are healed, run! Run with endurance the race set before you, continually trusting the Holy Spirit for that "secret power" that many before you have counted on to get them to the finish line. Run with endurance and keep running my friend. Don't look back; don't look to the left or to the right. Keep your eyes on the prize; keep your eyes on Jesus. God is faithful, and there is a great cloud of witnesses that are watching you as you reach milestone after milestone, winning victory after small victory, one step at a time.

> "Therefore, since we have so great a cloud of witnesses surrounding us, let us also lay aside every encumbrance and the sin which so easily entangles us, and let us run with endurance the race that is set before us, fixing our eyes on Jesus, the author and perfecter of faith, who for the joy set before Him endured the cross, despising the shame, and has sat down at the right hand of the throne of God."
> Hebrews 12:1-2

Run. Run my friend, there is a great cloud of witnesses from the entire Bible and church history watching. Run friend. Moses, Abraham, Joseph, King David, the Apostle Peter, the Apostle Paul, D.L. Moody, A.W. Tozer, and many more, including Jesus, the author and perfecter of your faith, are watching, and they are cheering you. So run. By His Spirit, you can do this. We need you to run.

I hope I have both encouraged you and challenged you. Thanks for riding along with me. May God bless you. Make sure to introduce yourself when you get to heaven after you have worshipped Jesus for oh say, a couple of thousand years. I am humbled and honored that you read this book. I can't wait to meet you in person.

> ". . . however, when the Son of Man comes, will He find faith on the earth?" Luke 18:8

CPSIA information can be obtained at www.ICGtesting.com
Printed in the USA
BVOW020142260912

301390BV00001B/4/P